Legacy of Love

My Education in the Path of Nonviolence

Legacy of Love

My Education in the Path of Nonviolence

ARUN GANDHI

NORTH BAY BOOKS
EL SOBRANTE, CALIFORNIA

Published by
North Bay Books
P. O. Box 21234
El Sobrante, California 94820
(510) 758-4276
www.northbaybooks.com

Comments and inquiries regarding this book may also be sent to
john@northbaybooks.com

Cover photograph shows Mahatma Gandhi (third from left), and
to the right, six-year-old Arun, Kastur, Manilal and Sushila
Gandhi. Photographer anonymous.

Manufactured in the United States of America.
Distributed by Publishers Group West.
Cover design by Elysium, San Francisco.
Printed by United Graphics, Mattoon, Illinois.

ISBN: 0-9725200-4-X
Library of Congress Control Number: 2003101191

First Printing: February, 2003

Contents

Publisher's Note

It is with gratitude that North Bay Books has published *Legacy of Love*. This book tells the story of Arun Gandhi's experiences, in South Africa and India, as he learned from his grandfather and parents the power and workings of nonviolence.

Part One, *Fundamentals*, provides background, showing episodes in the lives of Mahatma Gandhi and the author's parents that shaped the education Arun was to receive. Part Two, *Ashram School*, focuses on the lessons he absorbed as a youth in the presence of his grandfather, primarily during a stay at Sevagram Ashram that coincided with the last eighteen months of the Mahatma's life. It also includes episodes from Arun's childhood, in which his parents, Manilal and Sushila, demonstrated the wisdom of nonviolent parenting. Part Three, *Lessons From Life*, is a collection of observations drawn from Dr. Gandhi's application of the principles of nonviolence as an adult, in India and the United States.

We would like to acknowledge Amanda Lisle, Michelle Naes and Michael Nagler for their helpful roles in producing this work.

To my grandchildren,
Paritosh, Anish, Vivan and Kasturi

Introduction
A Grain of Wheat

It is not easy to write about my experiences with my grandfather, Mohandas Karamchand Gandhi, a man revered throughout the world for his simplicity and saintliness. I remember, for instance, when an article I wrote about my life with him appeared some years ago in an Indian magazine. The article was described as written by "Grandson, Arun Gandhi." A cousin chastised me at the time for what he considered to be blatant exploitation of our relationship. In fact, describing me as "Grandson" was not my idea. It was the editor who had insisted on this byline. But my cousin's criticism made me more sensitive to the issue, and for years afterward I felt it was best to hide my relationship with Grandfather. It was almost as though I was ashamed of being called "Grandson" of such a great man.

Later in life I began to ask myself why I should be reluctant to disclose my lineage. I recalled my mother Sushila's wisdom, which she imparted to her children as we were growing up. She told us, "There are two ways of dealing with it. You can either choose to be overwhelmed and live in Grandfather's shadow, or you can use the glow of his light to illuminate your path."

I eventually realized that Grandfather would not want us

to hide our true face from the world, but rather to share the lessons and the wisdom that we had learned. My father and mother, Manilal and Sushila, raised us to be compassionate, nonviolent citizens. I am grateful to have had such wise and loving parents, and also to have had the opportunity to live with Grandfather as a boy, between the ages of twelve and fourteen. Together, my parents and grandparents taught me the lessons that have shaped my life.

My parents lived what they wanted their children to learn. Nonviolence is based on five essential elements — love, respect, understanding, acceptance and appreciation — and they ensured that large measures of these sentiments were present in our home. Because I was raised with a sense of humility, I thought my experiences and understanding of the elements of nonviolence were of no special interest to others. However, I have learned that I was not only wrong, but also self-centered. If something has proved to be of so much good to me, it should be shared.

Grandfather once told me the story of a king in ancient India who became curious about peace. The king called upon many teachers and philosophers within his kingdom to explain its nature. None could give him a satisfactory answer.

Then one day a wandering sage stopped at the king's palace to pay him homage. In reply to the king's vexing question, the philosopher answered, "There is a wise man who lives just outside your kingdom. He alone can show you the nature of peace."

The next morning the king called upon the old recluse

who, when he heard the king's question, went into his kitchen and returned with a grain of wheat. Placing the grain of wheat on the king's outstretched palm he said, "Look here for your answer."

Too proud to admit that he was baffled, the king clutched the grain in his fist and hastily returned to the palace. There he found a little gold box and placed the grain of wheat in it. Each morning he would ritualistically open the box and look at the grain, but he found no answers there to his question. Weeks passed, and the king became increasingly disheartened. At last the wandering sage came again to visit the king, who promptly brought out the gold box and asked him to explain.

"It is quite simple, sire. As long as you keep this grain of wheat in a gold box locked up in your safe, nothing will happen. Eventually it will rot and perish. However, if you let the grain interact with all of the elements — air, water, sunlight — it will grow and multiply, and soon you will have a field of wheat.

"It is the same with peace," the philosopher continued. "If we keep the peace we have discovered in life locked up in our hearts, it will perish. But if it interacts with all the elements and all people, it will spread. And someday there will be peace throughout the world."

In keeping with this wisdom, I have decided to let my grain of wheat interact with the world. The stories that are shared in this book emphasize the importance of ethics, values and morals, and are intended to help us transcend the self-imposed, narrow-minded boundaries that restrict our understanding of the meaning of life.

Grandfather often said, "What we gain from academic studies is knowledge. What we gain from experience is wisdom." This book is the result of the hard-learned wisdom that was passed down, as a family legacy, from one generation of Gandhis to the next. Perhaps what people can learn through these stories is more lasting than what can be learned through textbooks.

Grandfather's last advice to me was to grow so that "your mind is like a room with many open windows. Let the breeze flow in from all directions, but refuse to be blown away by any one." My entire life I have tried to live by this dictum. It is with a profound sense of humility that I share these stories with you, in the hope that they will influence your life as they have influenced mine.

Arun Gandhi
Memphis, Tennessee
January, 2003

Part One
Fundamentals

First Class
Transforming Anger

"Get out, you coolie," the tall, rugged and angry white man barked.

"But I have a valid first-class ticket," the slight, sharply-dressed brown man said politely.

"I don't care what you have," the white man shouted. "If you do not get out now I will call the police."

"That is your privilege, sir. But I am quite comfortable in my seat," the brown man responded firmly, but without arrogance.

The angry white man huffed out of the compartment and moments later returned with a policeman and railway official in tow. The racist exchange was repeated, and then, finally, the three exasperated white men picked up the smaller man and literally threw him off the train. With smirks on their faces, they obligingly pitched his bags after him and signaled for the train to proceed to Johannesburg.

In spite of his impeccable manners, his polished British accent and his humble attitude, this little brown man was a victim of color prejudice. Circumstances, it is said, make the man, and the circumstances that converged in South Africa in the 1890s made this man—Mohandas Karamchand Gandhi—a political and spiritual leader of historic proportions.

This painful encounter at Pietermaritzburg railroad station in May, 1893 occurred just one week after my Grandfather had first arrived in South Africa. At the time he was, in effect, a young lawyer without a brief. He had absolutely no concept of nonviolence as a philosophy, nor that one day the world would venerate him as a Mahatma. The disgraceful episode drove him to an extreme of anger from which he was to emerge a new and enlightened man.

In the days and years that followed, experiences with color and race prejudices continually tested Grandfather's control of anger. The physical and psychological abuse that he endured would have driven most people to violent outbursts. There are instances throughout history where people who experienced a fraction of the suffering Grandfather experienced have been moved, through rage, even to kill. Grandfather, on the other hand, learned that the energy of anger could be used to create peaceful solutions that would affect the world in a far more positive way.

At Pietermaritzburg station, Grandfather's resistance to racism had only just begun. When he returned to India three years later, he wrote prolifically to inform politicians on the subcontinent about the plight of Indians in South Africa. He gave newspaper interviews and made pronouncements condemning the prejudicial policies of the South African government. When word of his efforts got back to South Africa, the local newspapers deliberately distorted his words, projecting him as an unconscionable threat to white rule. Such articles provoked paranoia, and created fears that Mohandas

Gandhi planned to import shiploads of Indians to eventually outnumber whites.

Consequently, when Grandfather sailed for a second time into Durban harbor, in January, 1897, together with his family and two shiploads of indentured Indian laborers, an infuriated mob waited for him on the pier. The South African government isolated the two ships in offshore quarantine, hoping the passengers and ship owners would eventually be forced to sail back to India out of frustration. A game of nerves was played out for nearly two weeks. The passengers waited patiently to disembark, and the mob waited to get their hands on Grandfather.

Dada Abdullah, the owner of the two ships, alerted Gandhi to the prospect of a violent reception. To protect his family, Grandfather formed a plan to send Grandmother ahead with their two boys (one of which was my father) to the home of his friend, Parsee Rustomjee, to await his arrival.

When the South African government finally realized that their effort to persuade the ships to sail back to India would not work, they permitted the ships to dock and the passengers, including Grandmother and her sons, to disembark. After everyone else had cleared the dock area, Grandfather, along with a white agent of the shipping company, left the ship, prepared to run the racist gauntlet. Naturally he was afraid, but submitting to fear is cowardice, and Grandfather despised cowardice more than violence. With great courage he began his walk, determined not to be provoked. He prayed for restraint to prevail, but the infuriated mob was ready to attack as soon as they saw him. They pushed the white agent aside and surrounded Grandfather. They began to beat him savagely, kicking and swearing in rage.

Though blood streamed down from the gashes on his head, Grandfather did not retaliate in any way. His peaceful response was not motivated by any articulated doctrine of nonviolence, but by a sense of reason. If he also resorted to violence, it would aggravate the situation.

It is quite likely the mob would have killed Grandfather that day if it were not for the fortuitous intervention of a white lady who recognized him and came to his aid. Mrs. Alexander was the wife of the police chief of Durban. She stepped between Grandfather and the frenzied attackers, and held her umbrella over Grandfather's bloodied head. Someone contacted the police, and they escorted Grandfather to the home of Parsee Rustomjee, where Grandmother and the boys anxiously awaited him. The mob followed, threatening to invade his friend's home if he did not surrender to mob justice.

The police chief tried to distract the crowd, even getting them to sing a song together, while his officers secretly smuggled Grandfather out of the house disguised in a police uniform. When word was received that Grandfather had safely arrived at the police station, the police chief told the mob, "Gandhi has mysteriously disappeared." By then the fiercest part of the crowd's anger had dissipated, and they quietly disbanded.

The police were able to identify and arrest a few of the

people who had attacked Grandfather that day. However, prosecution of the assailants required Grandfather to identify the suspects and file a complaint. Under similar circumstances, most of us would be eager to press charges. In today's world people are always seeking legal restitution. But such was not the case for Grandfather. He said he did not want revenge.

The police chief seemed even more surprised than the accused. He said to Grandfather, "I will have to release them if you do not file a complaint."

Grandfather replied, "That is fine. It's time we break this cycle of crime and punishment. They acted out of anger and ignorance, and if I do not forgive them, I will be as guilty of perpetuating hatred as they are."

Grandfather understood that his decision to forgive these men would liberate him from the burden of revenge and compel his opponents to evaluate their actions. He succeeded in planting a seed of doubt in their minds. Perhaps they had been wrong to attack this civil and compassionate gentleman. Having them repent was more important to Grandfather than having them imprisoned. He knew that placing them in prison would not teach them anything. Incarceration would only make them more bitter, and their prejudice would take deeper roots.

Even though he was a man of peace, Grandfather survived many such physical attacks while in South Africa, and at least eight assassination attempts during the time that he led the independence movement at home in India. I believe these episodes speak volumes about the depth of violence that exists beneath the surface of modern life.

In Johannesburg, Grandfather, as a representative of the Indian community, eventually signed an agreement with the government of South Africa to discontinue the mass protest campaign of Indian residents. Some Indians felt the agreement he had negotiated gained less from the government than they deserved. Doubters suspected that Gandhi had sold the interests of the Indian community for a price. Instead of questioning Grandfather and seeking clarification, they, too, became victims of anger and ignorance. One evening, three strapping, young Indian men waited for Grandfather to emerge from his law office, and then attacked him mercilessly. Thankfully, Grandfather was again saved by passersby, who took him to the hospital for treatment. Once more, when requested to file a complaint, Grandfather refused. The effects of unconditional forgiveness transformed his assailants. They realized their folly and all three showed their repentance by appointing themselves as Grandfather's bodyguards (even though Grandfather said he did not need any protection). They also became lifelong friends and followers.

Perhaps Grandfather's most unlikely convert to the path of peace was Khan Abdul Gaffar Khan, leader of a Pathan militia from the northwestern provinces of India. The Pathans were known throughout history as a warlike people. At the time they were engaged in a bitter and bloody conflict with the British. They felt "undressed" without their guns, and used them freely and frequently. When Khan Abdul Gaffar Khan heard of Grandfather's nonviolent struggle for independence, he was curious about the "tiny man" who expected to shake the British Empire without martial force. He had to meet him. Together with members of his revolutionary army, Badshah Khan traveled incognito to India's heartland to visit Gandhi.

People today wonder how a man of peace could welcome so warmly a man of such violence. This question arises because we look at everything as right or wrong, black or white, making no allowance for gray. We create divisions: Them and Us. This attitude contradicts the philosophy of nonviolence, which seeks to convert people through love and understanding, rather than by building walls between them.

Through a friendly dialogue based on respect and understanding, Grandfather changed Khan's violent ways and turned him into a revolutionary political leader as receptive and loving as India has ever known. Khan disarmed his militant group and converted them into a "Peace Army." Rejecting or denouncing men like Khan would have only created lifelong enemies instead of lifelong friends. The power of Grandfather's word and work overwhelmed others' hostility and anger because he was sincere, approachable and humble. He lived what he wanted others to learn.

Anger is a very powerful emotion, an emotion that, when misused or abused, has the capacity to create unimaginable and often devastating crises. As a result of society's ignorance and fear of anger, we have chosen not to explore its possibilities as a practical and constructive force. Each individual, consequently, finds his or her own destructive way of responding to anger.

Anger, however, is a force that can motivate individuals to good as well as evil. Angry at racist prejudices in South Africa, such as being thrown off the train because of the color of his skin, Grandfather was compelled to find a peaceful way to seek justice. Out of this and similar experiences he was able to gather the strength and persistence to formulate the principles of nonviolence.

Anger more often compels people to harmful actions, from saying things that destroy relationships to the extreme act of murder. When anger pushes people to such ends, they pay heavily for their folly, sometimes, as Grandfather saw too often, with their own lives. By misapplying anger we not only destroy our relationships with others, we also wound ourselves in ways that are difficult to heal. It is not difficult, however, to use anger intelligently, with self-discipline, and with better understanding and appreciation of its profound power. If we were not so ashamed of anger, we could easily learn to channel it into positive action.

Probably a hundred times during an average working day each of us is called upon to make decisions about the anger that we feel. Should we consume our lives with angry outbursts when faced with conflict, or would it be better to use the energy positively, so that we and those who surround us can learn and grow with experience?

Sometimes we make the right choice — we do want to resolve conflicts — but we go about it in the wrong way. We assume that by using the power of anger to intimidate, we can compel our opponents to accept our own, "correct" way of thinking. We do this with our children when we scold them, and with adults when we threaten or criticize them. Instead of resolving the conflict, these responses cause it to escalate. When words tumble out of our mouths with biting sarcasm, they cannot be retracted. Sometimes bullets fly out of guns with less damaging effect. In some cases we may defuse the situation by apologizing, nevertheless deep scars are usually left which serve as reminders.

We receive what we give. When we are disrespectful, suspicious, insulting or violent we will be paid back in the same coin. If we respect others as human beings, we rarely act rashly or irresponsibly toward them, and so we rarely have to say, "I am sorry." With thoughtfulness and respect for others in the presence of anger, we can channel anger into goodness, and make choices that heal, rather than aggravate, the divisions we encounter.

Seeds of Life
The Wisdom of Women

It is not true that highly educated and learned people are the main sources of wisdom. It often comes from children, and from people without privilege or formal education. Grandfather had little love for the scholastic education he received in schools and colleges in India and in England, which, he said, offered nothing but "book knowledge."

Schools, he believed, should lead us not only to knowledge of facts, but also to wisdom. If the knowledge attained in schools does not equip the individual to translate their experience into wisdom to live a better life, then, according to Grandfather, that knowledge is not worth much. Education today, as in Grandfather's time, is about being successful in a career and making money. It does not incorporate lessons in how to deal positively with one's emotions, or how to build better relations with others, nor does it teach how to let compassion guide our thinking so that we can create a cooperative society rather than a cruelly competitive one.

Grandfather used to tell a story from Indian scripture of a king who sent his only son to acquire the highest and best education available. The son came back with a lot of knowledge and an equal amount of arrogance. He thought he knew everything, and that he was wiser than others.

One afternoon the king summoned his son. "Have you learned how to know that which is unknown, and how to fathom that which is unfathomable?" the king asked.

"No, I haven't. How are these things possible?" the son asked.

The king said, "Go to the kitchen and bring me a fig."

When the son returned with the fig, the king said, "Cut it in half and tell me what you see inside."

"Lots of fig seeds," the son replied.

"Cut one of the seeds in half and tell me what you see inside," the king said.

"Nothing," said the son.

"That is correct. Yet, from that which you consider nothing, a huge tree emerges. That 'nothing' is the seed of life. When you learn what such nothingness is, your education will be complete," the king explained.

To save humanity from what appears to be certain disaster, we need to understand this "nothingness" and, in fact, reduce ourselves to this nothingness. This will bring us closer to Truth, help humanize our relationships, and teach us to respect people without conditions.

There were three people without formal education, all women, whose experiences with Grandfather influenced him as he grew up. The first woman who had a strong influence on him was his mother, Putliba. She could neither read nor write, and she had never seen the inside of a school. But she had a store of wisdom that came from life experience and the foundation laid by her parents.

Putliba was honest and pious, and had an almost insatiable thirst for spiritual knowledge. Although she was a devout Hindu, she was eager to learn about other religions and spiritual practices. She was, for her time, extremely open and inclusive. More through her actions than through direct instruction, she instilled in Grandfather the need for commitment and discipline in life — not the discipline of the military, enforced by orders, but the inner discipline that comes through spiritual awareness.

She not only prayed regularly, but she translated her prayers into practice and lived them. Putliba had compassion and respect for everyone. She regularly took vows as a form of spiritual discipline. Her vows often tested her resolve to the utmost, but the one that disturbed Grandfather the most was a vow she once made to fast until she saw the sun. Ordinarily such a vow would be innocuous enough, since we see the sun almost daily. However, his mother took this vow during the monsoon season in India, when the sun often could not be seen for several days. This meant she wouldn't eat for days on end.

Putliba cheerfully attended to all her chores, including cooking and feeding the family, without complaining or becoming irritable. That, she always said, was the essence of taking a vow. We must accept the consequences cheerfully. But Grandfather was a little child and devoted to his mother. He could not bear the thought of his mother suffering such deprivation while the rest of the family enjoyed their meals.

He would sit at the window for hours, peering into the sky and praying for the sun to break through the clouds so that his mother could eat. Sometimes his prayer would be answered. He would excitedly shout for his mother to come to the window at once and take a peek at the sun. By the time she came to the window the sun would hide behind the clouds, and his mother would smile and say, "It seems God does not want me to eat today."

Putliba used to tell her children, "A mind that is out of control is a devil's workshop." We see the effects of our "uncontrolled" minds today when we succumb to all kinds of temptations. For instance, we cannot do without many things that we know are bad for our health because, we tell ourselves, we are "hooked." Taking vows and learning to live without certain things in life are ways of taking control of one's mind. The idea is to give up, for a period of time, something that you are fond of, and then tenaciously hold to your commitment. Such vows are usually taken in a place of worship, with God as a witness, so that if you break them you are not just betraying yourself, but God also.

This attitude of service and sacrifice, for the self and for others, and performing these acts with a smile, had a great impact on Grandfather. His lifelong pursuit of higher spirituality, the power of prayer, and the discipline and sincerity involved in seeking Truth find their source in these early experiences with his mother.

Late in life Grandfather wrote,

The purer I try to become, the nearer to God I feel myself to be. How much more should I be nearer to Him
when my faith is not a mere apology, as it is today, but
has become as immovable as the Himalayas and as white
and bright as the snows on their peak?

As he grew up, Grandfather realized the importance of
taking and observing vows in order to reach purity of faith.
The vow of fasting, for example, teaches us that we need not
be slaves to food, that if we can master our sense of taste and
the craving for food, we will be better off physically and spiritually. He considered discipline in general, but the discipline
of the palate in particular, essential for the understanding
and practice of nonviolence, which calls upon one to suffer
all kinds of discomforts and privations in the interest of win-
ning justice and transforming an opponent's heart.

The second "unlettered" woman who taught Grandfather
powerful lessons was his baby-sitter, Rambha, who was nearly
the same age as his mother. As a child, Grandfather was as
fearful as he was rambunctious. Rambha had to be hired because Grandfather had a penchant for wandering and getting
lost. He also had a chilling fear of thieves and snakes, which
sometimes came to him in nightmares, and he would never
enter a dark room. His fears made Rambha's life as a baby-
sitter difficult.

Once she told him, "If you believe in Lord Rama, he
will always protect you. Whenever you are overcome by fears,
chant his name."

Grandfather practiced Ramanama, the silent recitation of God's name, diligently for the remainder of his life, and was thereby able to master his fear.

As an adult Grandfather learned that overcoming fear, both imagined and actual, is essential for the practice of nonviolence. We are controlled by fear because we submit to it, and unless we learn to overcome it in a positive sense we will always be oppressed. As he explained, overcoming fear in a positive sense means overcoming the fear of losing our comfort, possessions and attachments. Overcoming fear in a negative sense means charging ahead recklessly. Endangering one's self merely to show that one is not afraid is not the type of fearlessness that Grandfather advocated.

In the practice of nonviolence, one must not submit to injustice out of fears of losing a job or social position or property. Also, as in violent warfare, one must be willing even to sacrifice one's life for justice. Grandfather wrote, "I am prepared to die, but there is no cause for which I am prepared to kill."

The third "uneducated" woman to teach Grandfather a profound lesson was his wife, Kastur. They were both thirteen years old when they were married. The ill effects of child marriage became clear to Grandfather and Grandmother in adult life, and together they worked to end this practice in India. They never regretted having married each other, but they regretted the age at which they were betrothed.

At the time, Grandfather thought it was exciting to have

a playmate, especially if it was a playmate he could bully. What troubled him, however, was Grandmother's fearlessness and bravery. She was not troubled by darkness, nor did she dream of snakes and thieves. This made Grandfather feel inferior.

Shortly after their marriage, Grandfather became concerned about the issue of control. Specifically, who was to be "the head of the household," and how would that power be enforced? To resolve this issue he began reading books and pamphlets on the subject. Everything he read advocated that the husband lay down the rules of the house and enforce them strictly.

One night, emboldened by the advice he found in his sources, Grandfather told Grandmother as sternly as he possibly could, "From tomorrow, you will not step out of this house without my permission. Is that understood?"

Grandmother did not respond. She smiled and quietly went to bed. Just to make sure she had heard him, Grandfather repeated his warning, and still she said nothing.

Grandfather and Grandmother lived within the Indian joint-family system. In this arrangement, many generations live under one roof, with the eldest recognized as the patriarch or the matriarch, as the case may be. In such joint-family homes, the women and men tend to perform their duties separately. During the day the interior rooms of the home, generally, are the domain of women, where they do daily chores in the absence of men, while the outer rooms are occupied by men conducting business and hosting male guests. The only time that men and women come together is during mealtimes and at night.

Grandmother observed the next day that none of the other women sought their husband's permission to go out. She decided she was not going to do so either. She went out with the other women of the house, and not once did she ask Grandfather for permission.

A few days later, Grandfather angrily accosted Grandmother, saying, "How dare you disobey my order! Did I not tell you that you are not to stir out of the house without my permission?"

"Yes, you did," Grandmother said. "But please help me resolve my dilemma. My parents taught me that children must always obey their elders. I believe that in this house our elders are your parents. Now are you telling me that I should not obey your mother when she tells me to go outside, and obey you instead? If that is the case, I am going to tell her tomorrow that I will no longer obey her."

Grandmother expressed no anger, but there was firmness in her voice. Grandfather was dumbfounded. How could he tell his wife not to obey his mother? Knowing Kastur the way he did, he was sure that she would not hesitate to tell her mother-in-law that she had been ordered to no longer obey her. The issue was never brought up again.

Later in life, Grandfather sometimes called this his first lesson in nonviolent response. Ordinarily, given a similar situation, a person would have responded with anger, causing the conflict to escalate into a crisis. The calm and resolute manner in which Grandmother responded to the situation is essential to constructive nonviolence.

In his autobiography, *The Story of My Experiments With Truth*, Grandfather writes rather derisively about the carnal desires that made his father, Karamchand, marry for the fourth time when he was in his late forties. Putliba was a young girl when she and Karamchand were married. She bore him three sons, while his earlier three wives, whom he had lost by death, had two daughters among them.

Since women did not take an active role outside the house in the mid-1860s, Putliba encouraged her husband, who was prime minister in Rajkot and then in Vankaner, to invite religious leaders home so that she could learn from them about their practices. These discourses became regular affairs, and although Putliba could not come out and sit with the men and participate, she sat unobtrusively in another room where she could hear their discussions.

Seeing his mother forced to hide her intellectual curiosity because of her gender inspired Grandfather to work to liberate Indian women from their cultural shackles. He always fostered a healthy respect for women. He said, "As long as fifty percent of the population remains under subjugation, political freedom will be meaningless."

Grandfather insisted that women come out of their kitchens and become equal partners in the struggle for India's freedom from British imperialism. At public meetings and after prayer sermons he admonished men for treating women like chattel and, worse, treating them as objects of sexual passion. Indian society in his time, similar in many ways to the modern West, had frozen at a point where compassion and love had become synonymous with weakness and timidity. A male-dominated society had for too long branded women as the "weaker sex."

The oppressed, Gandhi observed, added to their burden of oppression by accepting the myths created by those who sought to dominate, and he urged women to break out of that mindset. He argued that they would not be liberated as long as they submitted. "No one can liberate you," he said, "until you liberate yourselves."

Grandfather succeeded in persuading many women to participate fully in the independence movement, and even to face the hardships of jail as a result. It meant spending a great deal of time and energy on a cause that many contemporary political leaders felt was a distraction. They claimed that the emancipation of women and "untouchables" were issues that could be better tackled after independence, by the government of a free India. But oppression from any source, Grandfather answered, cannot and should not be tolerated even for a moment. The liberation of women and the liberation of the low castes, he said, were issues that could not wait.

Modern women (and men) may take umbrage at some of Grandfather's statements about the sexes. Grandfather said that equality between men and women does not mean that women should aspire to do everything that men do. Men, he said, are more highly endowed with physical strength, while women have a greater natural store of compassion and spirituality. Although it may seem to some like a rash generalization, I don't believe it was. His observation had its roots in a

Hindu tradition that believes that there are two sides to a human being — one that is physically strong and another that is morally and spiritually strong. The physically strong side is most often activated when a person is moved by anger and fear, while the spiritual side emerges when one is moved by love and caring.

This dual nature is true of men as well as women, but the proportions of compassion and brute force embodied in each are different. I am very aware that some women today regard this view as heretical. I have been drawn into warm debates on this question, but no one has yet been able to convince me that it is incorrect. Grandfather believed that each of the sexes should build on the strengths they naturally possess.

"Most importantly," Grandfather urged women, "do not allow men to treat you as sex toys made for the pleasure of man. Men, too, will be able to liberate themselves only when they break the shackles of outdated tradition and learn to look at women with respect and dignity as equal partners rather than as sex-pots."

In modern life, sex dominates people's lives to such an extent that it has become a cultural obsession. Mass media bombards us with erotic images, and marketers blanket us with offers to enhance our sexual pleasure. Grandfather was not opposed to the enjoyment of healthy sexuality. But he sought to break the obsession that destroys our humanity and makes us lose the respect that we have for one another. He was equally critical of obsessive eating and drinking, and compulsive work habits.

Grandfather could never be accused of making a pronouncement that he did not first put into practice in his own life. In the ashrams [spiritual communities] that he founded, sexual relationships were prohibited, even between married couples, because the ashram was conceived as a unique, experimental school where everyone must participate in the eternal search for Truth. In order to break down old taboos and traditions men and women in the ashram had to work collaboratively, without sexual tensions and attachments. He advised those who wanted to lead a normal married life to live outside the community.

Grandfather saw the ultimate goals of life as being self-enrichment, self-purification and spiritual growth. He viewed sex, just like work, wealth and leisure, as one rung of a high ladder that each of us must master to become better human beings. The way to spiritual attainment and ultimate salvation is not defined by the number of times we go through the motions of praying, but by the discipline that we have in every aspect of our lives, by the continuous attempt to build our moral and spiritual strength, and through humility and truthfulness.

Climbing the Mountain
Religious Faith and Freedom

Grandfather used to say that religion is like climbing a mountain that has just one summit. If we are all going to the same place, why should it matter which side of the mountain one chooses to climb?

For generations, the Gandhi family has been more spiritual than religious. This may seem to be a contradiction, but it is not. The Gandhis have drawn a clear distinction between the two terms. Spirituality refers to the aspiration of all people toward an understanding and experience of our true nature, and ultimate realization of the Self. Religion, on the other hand, has in many cases come to mean a dogmatic observance of rituals that one practices at specified times of the day or week. For many people, religion in this sense seems to give them liberty to do as they please the rest of the time. Religion accentuates the distinctions between different traditions. Distinctions lead to comparisons, which lead to competitiveness, which leads to conflict.

At least from the time of my great-grandparents, Karamchand and Putliba Gandhi, our family has been open to all different philosophies, and has tried to learn about other faiths of the world without judgment. "A friendly study of all scriptures is the sacred duty of every individual," Grandfather always told us.

His respectful attitude toward all beliefs had its roots in the atmosphere in which he grew up. His parents regularly invited proponents of different religions to participate in friendly and open dialogue in their home, so that each could learn from the others. The phrase "friendly and open dialogue" should be emphasized here. These gatherings were not debates or comparative studies. Although one's view of the world is always tinged by the color of the glasses one wears, they nonetheless helped foster a deeper understanding of different religious practices, and respectful relationships among adherents of different belief systems.

Grandfather admits to having had an early bias against Christianity. As a child, he often encountered overzealous missionaries who stood on Indian street corners denouncing Hinduism as superstition. At that age, he says, he was moved to anger and rejected Christianity outright. He could have lived with that bias all his life, but he later realized that to reject anything out of anger was dangerous.

As an adult, he studied Christianity with as open a mind as he did all other religions. He concluded that no religion was perfect — none had answers to all the vexing questions that overwhelm us. This did not mean to Grandfather that we should reject our native religion because it is imperfect. He believed that we should cultivate the openness to seek Truth from all, and then incorporate into our own what is good. By drawing from other traditions and cultures we do not diminish our own faith; we enhance it. If this philosophy is acceptable in education, science and many other aspects of life, why should it not work in religion also?

Among those who became close associates of Grandfather was G. Ramachandra Rao, "Gora," an unusually garrulous atheist. He often came to Sevagram Ashram, near Wardha, where Grandfather lived toward the end of his life. At first Gora seemed to enjoy arguing with others in the ashram about God and spirituality. I was present one day, however, when Gora provocatively declared to Grandfather, "I do not believe in God."

Grandfather's responded calmly, "You may not believe in God, but can you say you do not believe in Truth?"

"Of course I believe in Truth," Gora replied.

"Well, then I believe Truth is God."

Gora was visibly moved by these words, and never criticized Grandfather's spirituality again.

Gandhi defined his life as being a diligent and faithful "pursuit of Truth," a conviction which is distinctly opposed to the common view that one's faith holds all the answers, and that one can thereby "possess the Truth." Truth, according to Grandfather, is the realization of the Self. We can reach this ultimate stage in life only by traveling a difficult road paved with humility and sincerity.

The assumption that someone already possesses the truth implies that he or she has achieved Self-realization, and thus embodies salvation. This assumption inhibits an individual's spiritual growth, and consequently, a person remains trapped in ignorance. From this comes the forlorn cry for the Divine to save our souls.

Grandfather would explain this folly by using the analogy of a swimmer who jumps into a river, certain that he can swim across, only to find the currents overwhelmingly strong. He cries for help and a lifeguard comes to his rescue and saves him. The lifeguard warns him of the dangerous currents, but the man is quite sure of himself. Instead of heeding the lifeguard's warning, he jumps in again the next day. Once again, the man is in trouble, and once again the lifeguard saves him. But the man is incorrigible. He refuses to learn from his actions, and keeps jumping into the waters until the lifeguard gives up and leaves the man to fend for himself. Mankind today emulates this man by persisting in violence and self-interest, and expecting to be rescued by the intervention of the Divine.

Religious philosophies today are sometimes translated and interpreted by human beings with the intent to exploit and control others. Instead of generating compassion and love, spiritual leaders speak of intolerance and violence against nonbelievers. Consequently, we have witnessed the worst forms of abuse — racism, oppression, wars and holocausts — in the name of God. If we as human beings despise hate, prejudice and violence, how can we accept such negative and abusive behavior as consistent with the Divine? Grandfather saw these errors at work in his own time, and shunned established religious institutions, saying that "they have become hotbeds of intrigue, prejudice and violence."

Grandfather arranged daily worship services that were inclusive of Hindu and non-Hindu expressions of faith. He included hymns from all major religions of the world, and the congregation was made up of people from many spiritual traditions. Prayer meetings were held outside in the open, or in a room that could accommodate a few hundred people but had no religious symbols of any kind. These services were held wherever he was, at specified times in the morning and evening, so that anyone interested could participate. People came in the hundreds, sometimes even thousands, from all walks of life.

It was Grandfather's effort to bring people of faith together, more than anything else, that gave many Muslims the courage and confidence to remain in India in spite of the creation of the Muslim state, Pakistan. Arrogant British Viceroys, conservative elements in the British home government, and ambitious and exploitative leadership among Hindus and Muslims had conspired together to poison the minds of Indian citizens so that the dismemberment of their country, in 1948, became inevitable. It broke Grandfather's heart to see that their poison acted faster and more comprehensively than his message of love and compassion and understanding.

The leader of Pakistan, Mohammed Ali Jinnah, and the British conservatives claimed that Hindus and Muslims could never get along. Yet if this were the case, one may well ask why two thirds of Indian Muslims chose to remain in India after the country was divided, despite the ruthless violence used to instill fear in the minds of the people.

The trouble between Hindus and Muslims, which has continued to this day, is not generated by the people's inability to get along, but by those in positions of power and influence who seek to exploit religious differences for personal gain. Those who continue to harbor ancient hate and prejudices in this way are only corroding their morals and values, leading to the ultimate destruction of their humanity. "Hate," Grandfather said, "is as corrosive as acid, and eventually destroys the vessel in which it is contained."

For Grandfather, religious unity and the abolition of the caste system, which is closely associated with Hinduism, were as important as political freedom for the country. He had people working in both of these spheres, which often irked his colleagues in the Congress Party. They complained that Grandfather was dissipating his energy on issues that should be tackled after independence.

"Political freedom will be meaningless," Grandfather replied, "so long as we continue to oppress our own people."

Grandfather was also aware that 98.5% of the political leaders and officials who would inherit the government of India when the British left were from the two upper castes— the Brahmins and the Kshatriyas. It was unlikely that they would be as zealous for reform as Grandfather was, since they enjoyed the power and privilege that the caste system gave them. Perhaps this explains why Grandfather often talked about wanting to live for one hundred and twenty-five years. He said he had so much to accomplish in order to make India into a land of peace, harmony and nonviolence that he needed at least that much time to reach his goal.

While Grandfather was firm about the need for Hindu reform, he was equally sensitive to the dangers of religious proselytizing. Religion, he would say, is like a mother. Whatever the mother's nature, one can criticize her, but not deny her. People's bond with the faith of their birth should be as strong as their bond with their mother. The religious bond must be as strong as the biological bond.

Many of those who work today to reform Hinduism are disappointed by Grandfather because they feel his approach was ineffectual. They would have preferred more aggressive methods. But such methods, Grandfather believed, are violent in nature, and rarely, if ever, achieve the desired results. When they appear to have done so, the results are only temporary.

Even though the reforms achieved by Grandfather are considered by some as insignificant, it is noteworthy that the Brahmins of his time felt sufficiently threatened to have masterminded eight attempts on his life since the first time he spoke against the caste system, in the late 1920s. Indian politicians, bureaucrats, and the Hindu citizen group that eventually assassinated Grandfather in 1948 attributed his murder to his so-called bias towards the Muslims. This is not true. His opponents acted in order to preserve the caste system. They conspired to make a martyr of Gandhi so that they could exploit his image, while no longer having to deal with his interference in affairs of State.

For professional politicians and bureaucrats, there was an additional reason for wanting Grandfather eliminated. He did not want Indians to step into British shoes and continue with British repressive policies. Grandfather talked about the need for simplicity. He spoke of converting the mansions and palaces built by the British into public institutions, and eliminating conspicuous consumption. Had he lived, Grandfather would have ensured that the Indian politicians and bureaucrats who replaced the British did not inherit their palaces and indulge in their frivolous pomp and pageantry.

There are two stories of faith that influenced Grandfather profoundly, and which he liked to share often with others. Both stories, I believe, shed light on how his spiritual beliefs empowered him to pursue justice with patience and courage.

In the first, there was an argument between the Divine and the Demon on the question of people's sincerity and faith. The Demon argued that people have faith in the Divine only as long as the going is good, but that in moments of adversity faith quickly disappears. The Demon challenged the Divine to test this theory on anyone that he chose. Raja (King) Harish Chandra, a legend in his lifetime and known for his honesty, integrity and piety, was chosen for the test.

The story of Harish Chandra resembles the Biblical story of Job. Raja Harish Chandra was subjected to unimaginable hardships, including the loss of his kingdom, his wife and his only son. He was made to work in a crematorium handling dead bodies, which was considered the lowliest of all work.

In spite of the worst kind of hardships, the Raja's faith remained steadfast. Finally, the Demon conceded defeat and the Raja was reinstated.

There are times in our lives when we feel the Divine is putting us to a test. "When this happens to you," Grandfather advised me, "remember this story of Raja Harish Chandra and never lose faith."

The second story, also from Hindu mythology, concerns the five honorable and honest brothers known as the Pandavas, who became victims of the evil designs of their cousins, the wicked Kauravas. The Kauravas challenged the Pandavas to a game of chance. Over a period of time, through dishonest play, the Kauravas were able to strip the Pandavas of everything they owned.

The taunting Kauravas challenged the Pandavas to a final throw of the dice — double or nothing. In desperation the Pandavas decided to wager their young and beautiful wife, Draupadi, the only woman in their lives. Once again, the Pandavas lost.

In the presence of the Pandavas and the assembly of spectators, the Kauravas decided to humiliate Draupadi and the Pandavas. Draupadi was dragged onto a stage where one of the Kauravas began to remove her sari. Draupadi stood trembling with fear as the cloth was unwound, one hand desperately clutching her sari and the other raised toward heaven, imploring the Divine to save her from this humiliation.

The Divine and his consort watched from heaven.

"Well, are you just going sit here and watch the spectacle?" the consort asked angrily.

"She doesn't seem to need my help," the Divine mused. "She still has faith in her own ability to hold her sari in place."

The Kaurava continued to pull at her sari, now with irresistible force, and in utter desperation, Draupadi raised both hands to heaven, imploring the Divine for mercy, placing her fate utterly in his hands. Mysteriously, the six-yard-long sari became endless. The evil man kept pulling and pulling at the fabric, but it continued to unwind, infinitely long, revealing nothing. The evil intentions of the Kauravas failed because Draupadi had put her full faith in the Divine.

The moral of the story, said Grandfather, is that our faith must always be absolute and unconditional. So long as Draupadi clutched her sari with one hand and pleaded for help with the other, she was indicating that she did not have full faith in divine justice. It was only when she stopped trying to save herself and put complete faith in the Divine that she was rescued.

Family Circle
The Scope of Unconditional Love

The spiritual communities that Grandfather founded and led, first in South Africa and later in India, were microcosms of what he hoped the world might eventually become. They were laboratories for experiments in human relationships, where people with differing philosophies and cultural backgrounds came together to live as a common family. Grandfather realized that such a society was essential for the success of a nonviolent revolution.

The concept of ashram life, like so much of Grandfather's thought and work, was borrowed from ancient tradition and modified to meet the needs of his time. Ashram schools were once prevalent in India, and, as a rule, were located in secluded areas in order for students to be close to nature and free from urban pressures. The schools were centered on a guru who selected his disciples carefully, and only those who had been carefully tested were admitted. Grandfather adjusted this concept by turning ashrams into centers for social change and places for developing a more perfect way of life. His ashrams emphasized a holistic, restorative process, which included social, spiritual, moral, political and educational elements.

Influenced by nineteenth-century social commentator and art critic John Ruskin, author of *Unto This Last,* Grandfather decided that if nonviolence is the goal, simplicity must be the way to achieve it. When, in 1904, he established his first ashram at Phoenix Farm, near Durban, South Africa, he invited anyone who was interested in the experiment to join the family. At first only his immediate relatives and a few cousins and nephews joined him. Then came friends and strangers. Grandfather put his ideas of simplicity into practice and, as he says in his autobiography, every day brought him new revelations of the power of nonviolence.

This experiment became an essential part of Grandfather's life, and so it was replicated at Tolstoy Farm near Johannesburg, also in South Africa. Later, when he relocated to India, it was repeated first at the Borsad Ashram, then the Sabarmati Ashram near Ahmedabad, and finally at the Sevagram Ashram in Wardha, central India.

In each of these ashrams, hundreds of people came together to live in cooperation. Everything was done in common — cooking, cleaning, farming, animal husbandry, building and, perhaps most notably, cleaning bucket toilets. This was a multifaceted experiment designed to break down taboos and prejudices, and inculcate in the participants a new sense of respect for and understanding of others. Like all experiments, this one, too, had its challenges. Overcoming centuries-old divisions and sensitivities was not easy. It needed almost superhuman effort.

The experiment was undertaken in the spirit of the proverbial thousand-mile journey that must begin with a first step. Grandfather knew that he was engaged in a social revolution that would take several generations to succeed, but a beginning had to be made. Whether Grandfather's experiment is to have its ultimate effect or not, only time will tell. But, as he would say, no sincere and dedicated effort is ever wasted. Besides, he always believed we should not do things with the result in mind, but do them because they are right. The fruits of one's actions will come in time. When we perform an act so that someone will praise it, or when we want to see the results immediately, we are subject to disappointment.

At the ashram, no one was exempt from performing their duties unless they were ill. Grandmother and Grandfather observed the rules and participated in the chores just as others did. I recall that as Grandmother grew older, she was not in very robust health, and her ability to perform arduous chores diminished. Still she remained active, supervising and supporting in the kitchen.

One afternoon Grandfather was on a routine walk around the ashram grounds and happened to pass the kitchen. When he looked in he saw Grandmother cooking. This was unusual because at this point in her life she preferred to leave such physically demanding chores to the younger ladies. Grandfather was curious, and he stepped in to inquire.

"What are you making?" Grandfather asked.

"Our son, Ramdas, is going home today, and I thought I would make some sweets for him to take to his children," Grandmother replied.

"Do you make sweets for all the guests of the ashram to take to their families?" Grandfather asked.

"What do you mean?" Ba answered, somewhat surprised.

"I mean, do you treat all the people of the ashram exactly the same as you do your sons?" Grandfather explained.

Grandmother quickly realized her mistake and said, "I am sorry. What would you think if I increased the quantity of the ingredients and made sweets for everyone in the ashram?"

"Now there you are," Grandfather responded. "We will all look forward to a treat."

Societies are torn asunder today not because violence is human nature and cannot be eradicated, but because excessive materialism and capitalism have made people self-centered and territorial. Consequently, the love, compassion, respect, and understanding appropriate to social life are neglected. Individualism and independence are valued most. Does that make Grandfather's philosophy of caring for others without distinction archaic and irrelevant? I think not. 1 would hate to see the day when love, compassion, respect and understanding are erased from our public lives. Violence is the inevitable result when these qualities are forgotten.

Harilal, Manilal, Ramdas and Devadas, in chronological order, were my grandparents' four sons. The eldest, Harilal, was born in 1888, just before Grandfather went to England to study law. My father, Manilal, was born on October 18, 1892, in Porbandar, India, after Grandfather had returned from England with his degree. It is remarkable that two sons of the same lineage, with the same upbringing, experiences and opportunities, grew up to become such diametrically opposed personalities.

While Manilal was a responsible and devout citizen, father and husband, Harilal became an alcoholic and wasted his life. He blamed his fate on Grandfather for not encouraging him to pursue a formal education. Grandfather was also criticized by people wedded to conventional ways of thinking, who believed that a father should be most loyal to "one's own." They argued that he sacrificed his own family in order to embrace others. They use this explanation to justify Harilal's rebellion. But Grandfather raised four sons following the same principles. Three did not rebel, nor did they waste their lives. Harilal not only rejected his parents, but he later abandoned his wife and four children, as well. This makes it difficult for me to accept that his rebellion was due to Grandfather's failings. To more deeply understand Harilal's choices in life would require another book.

Grandfather preferred that his children be educated at home, hence none of the four brothers had conventional schooling. My father, Manilal, who early in life aspired to become a doctor, chose not to rebel. Instead, he redirected his desire to care for others by dedicating his life wholly to the cause of nonviolence. This was a vocation well-suited to his gifts and circumstances, and one that he never regretted.

In 1915, not only did Grandfather's health require him to live in the warmer climes of India, but he also decided that fighting for the rights of Indians in their homeland was more appropriate for him than fighting hate and prejudice in South Africa. My father was the only son of Grandmother and Grandfather who had committed his life to practicing and teaching nonviolence, so at the age of twenty-five he accepted the responsibility of remaining in South Africa and running the ashram. In 1927 he married my mother, Sushila, and together they had three children. My sister, Sita, was born in 1928, I was born in 1934, and Ela, my younger sister, was born in 1940.

Our family maintained a tradition of going to India every two or three years, after which we would return to South Africa with the renewed vigor and vitality needed to continue the work of nonviolence. Because the struggle against hate and prejudice was morally and spiritually draining, the time spent in India, especially the long dialogues between father and son, helped my parents refresh their spirit.

Nonviolence is not just a state of being where violence is absent or invisible. It is a conscious, active effort not to harm anyone morally, spiritually, physically, mentally, economically, socially, or in any other way. A practitioner of nonviolence must be always guided by compassion for all. Nonviolence is also not solely, or even primarily, called upon for resolving conflicts. As Grandfather wrote, "Nonviolence has to become a way of life. It is not something that one could wear in the morning and take off in the evening,"

My parents practiced nonviolence not only in their public life, but also at home. They showered their children with love and respect from infancy, so that our bond with them was based on love and respect, rather than obligation. They never punished us individually when we misbehaved. They imposed discipline through penance. Sometimes my parents would fast because of our own misbehavior, and we would feel guilty and remorseful. Sometimes penance meant that no one in the family would be allowed to see a movie for a specified period of time.

I recall that one time, when I was a young boy, my father bought a box of chocolates. I stole the box and secretly consumed all of the candy. When I was caught, Father decided no one in the household would eat chocolates for the next three months. He did this in order that we might learn that for the missteps of a single person, the consequences are suffered by all.

Ahimsa is a Sanskrit word that appears often in Grandfather's writings, usually translated as "absolute nonviolence," or simply, "nonviolence." For Grandfather it had a much broader meaning. He said the essence of *ahimsa* was actually "unconditional love." Unconditional love is what we received from our parents and grandparents. Our task, when we were ready, was to offer it, in turn, to the larger world.

Part Two

Ashram School

South African Odyssey
Racism and Revenge

My attention was once drawn to the wisdom of an unknown philosopher who wrote, "In the murkiest mud a beautiful lily grows." I think that these words are quite appropriate for the situation in twentieth-century South Africa. From the mire of racial prejudices emerged great men, such as my Grandfather Mohandas, my father Manilal, Chief Albert Luthuli, Nelson Mandela, and Bishop Desmond Tutu. As I grew up in South Africa it became clear to me that only a person with commitment and discipline could turn his or her ugly racist experiences into a powerful philosophy capable of changing people into better, caring human beings.

In the South Africa of the 1930s and 1940s, overt hate and prejudice were still an integral part of a nonwhite person's everyday life. How intensely one was insulted depended upon the shade of one person's skin and the depth of the other person's prejudice. Sometimes prejudice in South Africa plummeted to ridiculous lows. There were, for example, instances in which white South Africans found themselves embarrassed by temporarily classifying one of their own as "nonwhite" when he or she had gotten a deep suntan.

When I was ten years old, three white teenagers approached me one Saturday afternoon, insulted me and beat me up, apparently for some racist satisfaction. I was punched, kicked, laughed at and called names, then left bleeding on the sidewalk. While the ordeal lasted only a few minutes, the scars will remain forever. I vividly remember stumbling to my feet and running home in fear, crying and angry. I had barely recovered from this humiliating experience when, a few months later, I again became a victim of prejudice and hate, and was beaten up by a gang of black African youths in Durban. It is now more than fifty-five years since these incidents, but I can still see the hate-filled eyes of the young men, and feel the pain and anguish of every blow.

A related experience occurred when I was seventeen years old and decided to wait in the car while my parents and sisters went shopping along Durban's prestigious West Street. Commercial integration, at the time, was tolerated while social integration was not. We were parked near a whites-only bar that attracted all kinds of riffraff. As I waited I saw a drunken white man looking to panhandle so that he could buy more alcohol. Living in a hate-filled society forces one to develop an intuitive ability to sense potential conflict. The moment our eyes met I knew the encounter did not bode well.

The drunk unsteadily shuffled towards the car glaring toward me, and I quickly rolled up the windows, locked the doors and pretended to read. My fears were confirmed as the drunk began to pound on the window, shouting obscenities and demanding money.

"Hey, coolie, give me a bob!" he sputtered, using slang for a shilling. I ignored him. Again he yelled, this time with even more force and venom, and still I ignored him. In frustration, he spat on the window and walked off in disgust. I know that if the windows had not been not shut, he would have gladly spit in my face.

What made this event more disturbing was the presence of a white policeman close at hand, who watched intently to see whether or not I would react. I knew the policeman would be more interested in protecting the rights of the white alcoholic beggar than the rights of a nonwhite person. If I had retaliated, cursed in anger, or in any way insulted the white drunk, the policeman would have happily arrested me. On the other hand what the white drunk did to me was, to other whites, a cause for amusement.

To outsiders, the social conditions under which nonwhites lived in South Africa were unimaginable. As late as 1968 they remained blatantly cruel and unjust. It was during that year, while on a visit to South Africa, that Derek Ingram, an English journalist friend, sent word to me that he would be in Durban and asked if we could meet. I arranged to pick him up at his hotel so that we could spend the day together. As I walked up the steps to the front lobby, a white doorman asked rudely, "Where do you think you are going?"

"To meet my friend who is a guest in the hotel," I said politely.

"You wait here on the sidewalk," he said brusquely as he took Derek's room number and went in to call him.

Derek was on the line to London and, assuming I was comfortably seated in the cool lobby, took his time coming down. When he arrived in the lobby and could not find me, he walked out the front door and was shocked to see me standing uncomfortably outside in the sweltering summer heat.

"Why are you standing out here?" he asked.

"Welcome to South Africa," I said. "Nonwhites are not allowed to enter these hotels except as slaves of white masters."

This concept was inconceivable to Derek. He was livid, and insisted upon checking out of the hotel immediately. It took me a while to convince him that his efforts would be futile, since all the hotels in South Africa discriminated against nonwhites. The only way I could enter a hotel with Derek was if I was willing to carry his bags.

I recall reading an article published that same year in the *Natal Mercury*, a white-owned Durban daily, that widened my perspective on prejudice. The news piece told of a white policeman who entered a white Christian church for a routine check and found a black man kneeling at the altar.

"What are you doing here, *kaffir*?" the policeman barked.

"Mopping the floor, *baas*," the African responded, using a term of respect.

"Well, God help you if I catch you praying," the policeman warned.

Even God and Jesus were incorporated into the racist imbroglio of South Africa.

People who are forced to live under oppression develop a measure of tolerance, the level of which differs from individual to individual. Some develop the capacity to suffer greater insult than others. As a rule, therefore, most nonwhites in these environments play it safe and never confront or challenge a white person, whatever the provocation. In 1893, when my Grandfather first suffered racial prejudice and spoke about it to his Indian friends, they, at first, dismissed him as naive. They were businessmen, and they had learned to accept indignities and injustices in order to continue to make money.

"This is the reality of South Africa," they all said. "That is why we try not to be where the whites don't want us."

It was a shock to Grandfather to realize that people were willing to allow a system of hatred to perpetuate. It was something he was not willing to accept.

One might expect that in a diverse country such as South Africa, the solution would be for all nonwhites to join together to oppose white racism. But, as it turned out, South Africa was a patchwork of oppression. There was as much prejudice between the different groups of nonwhites as there was between whites and people of color. It seemed like everyone hated each other.

For many years after my South African odyssey I nursed scars of humiliation, and it has been difficult to come to terms with them. I seem to be more sensitive to the effects of these early experiences with racial bias than others. People like me often suffer from paranoia, seeing hate and prejudice in even the most innocent actions of others. Such people seldom, if ever, fully recover from the humiliation. I myself still suffer the aftereffects.

As a youth I naturally succumbed to the temptation to seek "eye-for-an-eye" justice. I was not endowed with the wisdom or the foresight to transform these violent racial experiences into positive action for justice. I simply buried the anger and humiliation deep inside of me and secretly vowed to someday get revenge. I joined a program of bodybuilding and weightlifting to prepare for the day when I would finally get my pound of flesh.

But the path I had chosen to seek justice was suicidal. While I was gaining physical strength I was losing my values and moral rectitude. I was becoming what I hated most. Anger was taking control of my being, and hate and violence were taking root. My increasing interest in vengeance eventually led my parents, who were naturally troubled, to make a decision that would change the course of my life. They knew that it was time for me to spend time with Grandfather, and learn the wisdom of his peaceful ways.

Sevagram Ashram
Simplicity and Community

My youthful obsession with physical strength and retaliation caused my parents understandable concern. As a result, they decided to travel to India as soon as possible to visit Grandfather and the extended family. Also, my grandmother Kastur had died in prison in 1944, and because of World War II my father had not been able to go to India and pay his respects. It was now 1945, the war was almost over, and the sea-lanes between South Africa and India had been reopened to civilian traffic.

A note about our home at Phoenix Farm, outside Durban: We lived there for many years in a house that Grandfather had built in 1904 out of corrugated iron and wood, with basic functional furniture. We sat on chairs and slept in beds. By 1943 the house was falling apart. The iron walls had rusted so that there were gaping holes at ground level, making it convenient for snakes and rodents to crawl in and out. The roof was like a sieve, providing very little shelter during the rainy season. It was nearly impossible to live there. The traffic of invading pests had increased substantially, so that getting up at night, in a pitch-black room without electricity, was quite a terrifying experience. Is there a snake near the bed? In the bathroom? Questions like these were incessant.

Shortly before our trip, we moved into a simple, spartan home, also in Phoenix, built with cement blocks and tiled floors. Compared to the old one our new home was luxurious. Nevertheless, I was ecstatic when I heard we were going to India. On our earlier visit, in 1940, I was only six years old, too young to appreciate Grandfather's charisma, philosophy, and the purpose of his struggle. Now, at the age of twelve, I was beginning to understand the relevance and importance of such matters. I was also wearied and frustrated by the racist climate of South Africa, so that the idea of going anywhere else seemed good enough for me.

It was on the tenth day after our arrival in India that we reached Sevagram Ashram, in the Indian heartland. The eighteen-hour train journey from Bombay to Wardha (the nearest rail station to Sevagram) was a thrilling experience. I had never before traveled such a long distance on a train with so many people. There was the added excitement of meeting the family, being with Grandfather, and seeing a country I had not visited since childhood.

For a first-timer, Sevagram Ashram would appear to be very remote, miles away from anywhere. I learned later that Grandfather chose this isolated location because he was always overwhelmed by teeming and noisy crowds, and seldom found peace or quiet. Sevagram was far enough from any major population center to dissuade people from visiting. Adding to the inconvenience of the journey to Sevagram, Grandfather had asked the authorities not to organize public transportation from the town of Wardha. This ensured that only those with serious purposes would come to meet and discuss affairs with him. To do so would require either a six-mile walk from the rail station, or an expensive ride in a taxi or horse buggy.

At Wardha station, father hired a horse buggy to carry my younger sister, Ela, and me with our bags, while he and mother would walk the distance.

"If you walk, I will walk with you," I said with a sense of bravado. I was at the age when a boy is determined to do everything his father does. At the back of my mind, I guess, I also wanted to show off to Grandfather that I was old enough to walk the distance, too. I had absolutely no idea what it meant to walk six miles on a dirt road in the scorching heat of central India. The dust, heat, thirst and hunger tested the limits of my endurance. At times I was sorely tempted to hop into the buggy, but I would not admit failure.

I don't know whether it was my family bias towards Sevagram, which was so closely linked in my mind with Grandfather, or whether everyone felt this, but as we approached the ashram, it appeared to wear an aura of serenity. It was as if we were entering a holy place. The ashram was not glamorous. It was the epitome of simplicity. Mud huts with thatched roofs of all sizes were spread over a broad campus. There were few shrubs and trees, and no lawns. It reflected the asceticism of Grandfather's philosophy. Not that he had anything against beautifying the surroundings, but he did not want anything to distinguish him from the poorest Indian. The village of

Sevagram, just a half mile down the road from the ashram, was very, very poor. If the ashram had manicured lawns and flower gardens, it would not only take a great deal of time and resources to tend, but it would also make it look grander than the village. This, Grandfather felt, would be just another unnecessary barrier between him and the people he served.

Our entrance into the ashram was unheralded. People knew we were coming, but the rule was that all comings and goings would be quiet affairs. We made our way to the hut occupied by my mother's uncle, Kishorelal Mashruwala, and his wife, Gomti, who were close associates of Grandfather. Later I learned they were also responsible for my parents' marriage. Their modest hut was close to the entrance of the ashram.

We washed and snacked, then ventured towards Grandfather's hut, which was no more than ten feet by ten feet, with a mud floor and a thatched roof. In a corner near the door Grandfather sat on a thin cotton mattress covered with a clean, white cotton sheet. Visitors squatted on straw mats on the floor. There were no fans, no lights and no other furniture. I had imagined Grandfather's home to be made of more sturdy material, with more furniture, and secretaries and attendants hovering around him.

As it turned out, Grandfather was not at all what I had imagined him to be. He was loving, effusive and extremely approachable. He had a way of disarming people and making them feel at home. From the moment I set eyes on him, I felt drawn to him, and I was filled with a sense of pride and belonging. I had expected that he would give us just a few minutes and then dismiss us so that he could attend to more pressing matters, but instead he exuded immense warmth and hospitality. The few people who were in the room when we arrived realized that this was a family moment and left. Following our parents, Ela and I stooped to touch our Grandfather's feet in the traditional Indian obeisance. He pulled us to him and gave us affectionate hugs and kisses.

I can still hear Grandfather's toothless laughter and see the twinkle in his eyes when he was told that I had walked from Wardha station to Sevagram. In appreciation he gave me a resounding thump on my back and said, "I am impressed." It was the greatest blessing I could ask for.

Later that day, when I heard that my parents had agreed to leave me at the ashram while they traveled around India visiting relatives and friends, I was delighted. Ordinarily one wouldn't be so elated to live with Grandfather, because it meant adhering to the strict rules and discipline of the ashram. I would have to eat plain food, and get up at four-thirty in the morning to attend the five o'clock prayer meeting. No one at the age of twelve would normally want to do any of these things. On reflection, I think I just enjoyed the thought of being at the center of the spotlight. The adulation that people poured on Grandfather, and all the eminent leaders who came to consult with him, made me feel honored to be his grandson.

During the first few days that I was at Sevagram, I could not help but be struck by the austerity of life there. In keeping with the culture of the country and the poverty of its people, Grandfather had adopted a radically simple life-style. I was too young to comprehend the significance of such frugality. Although such thoughts passed through my mind, I don't remember ever complaining. I was happy to be living there, like everyone else, and I was grateful for the absence of snakes (although, as I was told later, central India is the home of the deadliest cobras).

The Sevagram grounds were dotted with structures of all different shapes and sizes. There were more than 200 residents living there, some single and some living with their families. Meals were cooked in a large group kitchen, and everyone assembled to eat in a common dining area. Each person was responsible for bringing his or her own plate, cups, bowls and utensils, and had to wash them and put them away after each meal. All activities, from cooking to eating to studying to socializing, were done seated on the floor.

Cleaning the campus, working in the vegetable garden, and cleaning the public toilets — carrying buckets of urine and night soil to the fields and emptying them and washing them — was done by each person as part of a team. The teams rotated every week, and there was true gender equality. One could never say this is a woman's job or, conversely, this is a man's job.

Our first week at Sevagram Ashram caused us — especially my sister Ela and I — some anguish. We were warned that meals at the ashram would be bland, but we were unprepared for the three-times-daily dose of the same insipid food. It made me wonder if Grandfather was not stretching his concept of a simple life-style a bit too much. In Phoenix we were accustomed to plain, balanced, nutritious fare. There were fewer people involved, but I couldn't understand why that should make such a big difference. From the day we arrived at Sevagram, we were fed boiled pumpkin without salt or spices, and dry bread, day after day.

Because of the pressure of work and the need to take a prescribed diet, Grandfather did not eat with the rest of the community, so he did not know what we were fed. Everyone assumed that what was being cooked was under his instructions, and since no one wanted to appear to be weak, no one questioned the choice of vegetable. Suffering quietly is the essence of nonviolent action, and it was being practiced to perfection at Sevagram. There was, however, one person who seemed to be enjoying this predicament: Munnalalji, the person in charge of provisions and the menu.

Three days of this boiled pumpkin diet was more than Ela and I could endure. We complained to our parents but, like the others, they too believed that this was done under Grandfather's instructions. After all, we were visitors from South Africa and it would be inappropriate to start complaining right after our arrival. I was silenced, but Ela was only five years old and quite incorrigible. On the afternoon of the fourth day, without my parents' knowledge, she walked into Grandfather's room and said, "Bapuji, I think you should change the name of this ashram."

"Why?" Grandfather asked in amazement.

"Well, since the day we arrived, I have not seen much of
seva [service], but I have eaten a lot of *kola* [pumpkin]. So it
would be more appropriate to call this ashram 'Kolagram' instead of 'Sevagram.' "

Grandfather was intrigued. He put aside his work and
said, "Come here, my child, and explain in detail what you
mean."

Grandfather had the unique quality of dealing with everyone and every issue with the same seriousness. Nothing
was unimportant or insignificant. He treated Ela's complaint
with the same earnestness as he would a challenging question
posed by a politician concerning the freedom struggle.

"I am tired of eating saltless boiled pumpkin and dry
bread every day, and would love to eat something else for a
change," Ela said with childish candor.

"You are quite right," Grandfather said. "We must look
into this."

He promised Ela he would get to the bottom of the
problem as soon as possible. That evening, during his after-
prayer sermon, Grandfather shared Ela's complaint with everyone and called upon Munnalalji, who also managed the
garden, to explain.

"I was only following your instructions, Bapuji," he said.
"Did you not tell us we must eat simple, boiled food?"

"Yes," Grandfather replied. "I do advocate a plain diet,
but surely that does not mean eating the same food every day."

The truth then emerged. "We planted a whole field of pumpkins, and we have such a bumper crop that we do not know what to do with it all," Munnalalji confessed. "That is why we have been cooking so much pumpkin."

"That is bad planning," Grandfather admonished. "Why would anyone plant only pumpkins and no other vegetables?"

Munnalalji was told to find a solution in keeping with the policies of the ashram — no waste and no commercialization. The next morning Munnalalji loaded the ashram bullock cart with pumpkins, hauled them to the neighboring village market, and bartered them for other vegetables. Everyone heaved a collective sigh of relief and showered Ela with their blessings. Had it not been for her temerity, God knows how long we would have had to suffer boiled pumpkin — morning, noon, and night!

This episode illustrates how some followers approached Grandfather's teachings rigidly and dogmatically, sometimes distorting them to the point of making a mockery of them. Grandfather was aware that not all of his followers had the capacity to operate within a living philosophy that was continuously being tested and perfected. Although he was sometimes criticized for contradicting himself, Grandfather claimed that every day, through every incident, he was discovering new aspects of his faith. Since our understanding of Truth itself does not remain constant, one who is determined to pursue it diligently must constantly test and reexamine his or her views.

Beginning Lessons
Self-Control

Grandfather was aware of the racist attacks I had suffered in South Africa and the rage they had generated. He knew he had to speak to me about channeling my anger into positive action, but he waited for an appropriate occasion. He did not have to wait long. One day, upset by the behavior of another child as we played together, I went to Grandfather in tears. Seeing that an opportunity had come, he set his work aside to teach me what I still regard as the most important lesson I have ever learned: how to understand anger and use it wisely.

Grandfather was possibly the world's best teacher. He taught through the example of his own life, and by reducing his principles and practical wisdom into simple, understandable stories that even a young person could understand and appreciate. He often said that he learned more from the tales that his parents and teachers told him than from any of the books he had to memorize during his years in school.

"Bring your spinning wheel and come sit down with me," Grandfather said. I want to tell you a story." Spinning cotton required concentration and meditation. It was very soothing, and Grandfather often used it as therapy to focus his agitated mind.

"There was a young boy your age," the story began, "who

was always angry because nothing seemed to happen the way he wanted. The boy had his own agenda and his own perspective on everything, and because he was unwilling to recognize the value of other perspectives, he lost many of his friends. No one likes someone who is obstinate and prone to tantrums. The few who remained his friends took pleasure in provoking him and watching his angry outbursts.

"This went on for years, until the boy reached an age when his simple tantrums would break out into violent actions. One day he got into a very serious fight and accidentally committed murder. In one moment of thoughtless passion, he destroyed his own life by taking the life of someone else. This is what can ultimately happen when people allow themselves to give free rein to anger.

"Now is the time for you to learn to listen and to cooperate," Grandfather said. "There will always be another point of view besides our own — sometimes right, sometimes wrong — and we must develop the capacity to pause calmly and evaluate. Then we can take a stand that is not aggressive, but conducive to bringing about awareness and change. We must also cultivate the humility to acknowledge when we are mistaken, just as we expect others to acknowledge their own mistakes.

"When anger takes control of our minds, we become violent, shouting irrationally at each other, or worse. In these outbursts the casualty is Truth. The ability to respond to anger nonviolently will come to you through constant practice," he said. "Do not be domineering, always be fair and just.

Remember that being humble does not mean giving in and allowing yourself to be bullied. Humility means giving respect. You will have respect in return to the extent that you give it to others."

When Grandfather paused to attend to someone who came to make an inquiry I thought the day's lesson was over. I was eager to rejoin the other children, so I promised Grandfather that I would not do anything to precipitate another crisis and got up to leave.

"Wait a minute, young man, I am not quite done yet. We still need to talk about using anger constructively."

I was embarrassed to have my anger discussed openly and extensively. There was some inexplicable urge in me to project a good image of myself, not the image of a problem child. I had always thought anger was evil.

"Anger is good," Grandfather said, "and I am glad to see you can be moved to anger."

I thought he must be pulling my leg, but he was serious.

"Anger, you see, is to people what fuel is to an automobile. Without it, we would not be motivated to rise to any challenge, and life would be no more than mere existence. Anger is an energy that compels us to define what is right and wrong, good and bad, just and unjust."

"Anger is also like electricity," Grandfather continued. "Electricity is powerful — so powerful, in fact, that it can cause devastating destruction if it is mishandled or abused. But if channeled properly and intelligently, it is highly useful to mankind."

He then gave me a piece of paper, saying, "On one side of this sheet I want you to write all the useful applications of electricity you can think of, and on the opposite side all the destructive applications."

I set to work on the two lists, and it quickly became clear to me that it is almost solely through negligence or abuse that electricity becomes harmful to human life.

When my young mind could think of no more good or bad applications of electricity, Grandfather instructed me to follow the same formula, and jot down all the good and bad applications of anger. It turned out I could fill a whole page with bad applications, including violent ones, but I couldn't think of a single good one, because I had no idea yet how anger could be used positively.

Grandfather then explained that we can avoid all the evils that anger leads to if we regard it as a warning system that something is wrong. If we can control our thoughtless responses and pause to analyze the situation carefully, anger will provide the energy we need to think of ways to resolve disputes nonviolently, with positive results.

"From now onwards I want you to keep an anger journal. Every time you are moved to anger, stop and write down who or what caused your feelings and what the circumstances were — what was said and by whom and why. Most importantly, I want you create and write down a solution to each problem so that everyone is happy. Whenever you need help finding the right solution, come and talk to me. But before you come to me, I want you to exercise your own good judgement. If you do this regularly, it will build in you the habit of translating your anger into positive, nonviolent action."

This daily exercise transformed my life in substantial ways. Without it, I might easily have become sullen, emotional and embittered, inflicting enormous damage upon myself and those around me. Studying the implications of anger in this way also made me aware of how one violent person affects the lives of so many.

I want to emphasize here that learning to think and act nonviolently does not happen without great effort. For many generations we have been conditioned to respond to conflict with violence, and transformation cannot take place simply because we want it to. In my own case it required the discipline, each time I felt the presence of anger, to force myself to interrupt the process. Hard work and sacrifices are necessary if we are to, as Grandfather urged, "live what we want others to learn."

Thousands of people sought Grandfather's autograph, thus time was allotted every day to sign autograph books, after the morning and evening prayers. Being a practical person, Grandfather realized that selling his signature for five rupees (approximately five dollars today) would bring in much-needed revenue for his social and educational programs. To make the process more efficient, volunteers like myself collected the money together with the autograph books, which we brought to Grandfather to sign.

One day I was busy making myself a little autograph

book when Abha, my cousin's wife, dropped by and asked, "What are you doing?"

"I am making an autograph book so that Bapuji can sign it for me."

Abha laughed. "Do you have five rupees?"

"No," I said.

"Then you will not get the autograph," she said matter-of-factly.

"What do you mean?" I said with some indignation. "Am I not his grandson?"

Abha obviously knew Grandfather better than I did, but since she did not want to get into an argument she simply said, "All right, we will see what happens."

One evening in Pune, I slipped my autograph book into the pile that I took to Grandfather, silently praying that in the rush of the moment he would sign my book. I was sadly mistaken. Grandfather was absolutely meticulous about every dime that he received. He had to know exactly how much came in, as well as how it was spent. So, when he came to my book and saw no money accompanying it, he asked, "Why is there no money for this autograph?"

I said, "Because it is my book, Bapuji."

He smiled, "So you are trying to pull the wool over my eyes? Why do you need an autograph?"

"Because everyone has one," I said.

"Well, as you can see, everyone pays for the autograph," he replied.

"But, Bapuji," I pleaded, "I am your grandson."

"All the more reason why you must pay," he said.

"No Bapuji!" I became adamant, "I will make you give me an autograph for free."

Bapuji laughed and said, "Is that so? Well, let's see who wins this challenge."

In the days that followed I used every strategy I could think of to pester him for an autograph, to the extent that I would crash his meetings with high officials in hopes that he might sign the book just to get rid of me. He would not. When I became too insistent he would simply put his hand across my mouth, press my head against his chest, and continue with his discussions. This went on for weeks, until I realized I would never get the autograph, no matter what I did.

What amazed me most at the time was Grandfather's patience. He never lost his temper, nor did he tell me to get out of the room and leave him alone, as we would if our children disturbed us while we were involved in something important. In retrospect, what impresses me is Grandfather's firm adherence to his rules, and the control that he had over his anger in spite of my puerile attempts to provoke him. The degree of self-control that Grandfather displayed in everything he did made me realize that, if we could all cultivate a fraction of his discipline, it would help to substantially reduce the violence that consumes our societies around the world.

After this lesson Grandfather decided that he would spend an hour every day with me, talking and listening. With the busy schedule he had, I wondered how he would find an hour every day. I learned quickly that disciplined habits and proper use of time enable people to accomplish a lot more in one day than I had imagined. Spending time to teach me was a priority for Grandfather. To instill in me the discipline that he valued, Grandfather helped me prepare a daily schedule. This included play time, tutoring time, plus all of my ashram chores. My schedule was attached to the wall of my room for ready reference, and I was required to abide by it strictly.

Nonviolent Discipline
Penance and Humility

When we hear of discipline today it often calls to mind military schools and other authoritarian regimes. Some might look at life at Sevagram Ashram, which operated according to strictly observed rules, and compare it to a boot camp. But when one looks more closely one finds profound differences.

In the more familiar form of discipline, the emphasis is on control by fear. I recently conducted a workshop on nonviolence that was attended by high school teachers and counselors. To a surprising degree, even they rejected the idea of control through love and respect, which is the core principle of nonviolence. Many firmly believed the only way children can be disciplined is by using the "stick." One of them boasted to me, "I now just have to glare at the children and they obey."

"But what will happen when they grow out of that fear?"

"They dare not," she said firmly.

Not only is this teacher educating her children in violence, she also has to continuously escalate her own violence to keep control. Her method of teaching breeds disrespect and prejudice. Her students have been dehumanized.

Ashram life, on the other hand, was based on the belief that living together, sharing a common discipline rooted in love and cooperation, will help shape responsible and dignified human beings. Grandfather enforced discipline with a deep understanding of the principles of nonviolence. He kept an open mind, with respect for everyone, and was able to treat even his opponents with dignity and fairness.

Some people refer to Grandfather as a compassionate dictator, one who succeeds in getting his way through love. In a sense this is true. Whatever he asked you to do, it was very difficult to say no. But he often cautioned us about this kind of blind adulation, which could easily be exploited by someone less scrupulous.

Grandfather did, at times, display a stern attitude. Nevertheless, he was the joy of the ashram. During the few times that I stayed behind while Grandfather was on tour, I found the compound to be virtually lifeless, even though hundreds were still involved in the ashram routine. In his absence, I must confess, the ashram sometimes seemed like just another cooperative living arrangement, where you found yourself performing your duties mechanically.

In the ashrams that Grandfather founded, people of all colors, castes and religions worked together, ate together and worshipped together. Ashram prayer sessions were held every morning and evening, outdoors on an open ground on dry days, or in the large dining hall when it was wet. There were no religious symbols because Grandfather believed in the oneness of all religions. There were hymns from every major religion of the world, sung by everyone who was present.

What was most odious for many was getting up at four-thirty every morning in order to be washed in time for the five o' clock prayer service. It was important to Grandfather that everyone learn this discipline as a part of nonviolent living. Excuses such as, "I just could not get up," or, "I slept late," were not acceptable. The only time you were exempt from the schedule was when you were really ill. I remember an incident with Manu, my cousin, who was a teenager when she was living with Grandfather.

One morning she ignored the four-thirty wakeup bell. When she heard the footsteps of the other ashram residents walking towards the prayer ground, she sat up in bed and pretended to be getting ready.

"Are you ready?" Grandfather called out as he passed her room.

"Yes, Bapuji. I'll be there in a minute," Manu said.

Instead, she turned over and went back to sleep. An hour later, when Grandfather and the prayer party were returning, Manu heard their footsteps, scrambled out of bed and started brushing the long tresses of her hair.

"Why did you not come for the prayers?" Grandfather inquired.

"What can I do, Bapuji?" Manu lamented. "My hair is tangled so badly I couldn't get it straightened out in time."

"Now, that is bad," Grandfather said. "How can we allow tangled hair to come in the way of our communion with God?"

Grandfather did not punish Manu. He addressed the problem in a practical way. Manu's hair was cut shorter, so that, in the future, caring for it would not make her late for prayers.

A recollection from an earlier visit to Sevagram, in 1939 when I was only six years old, illustrates another aspect of Grandfather's form of discipline.

While we were staying with my grandparents at the ashram I became friends with a boy named Anil, who was my age. Anil had a weakness for sweets that verged on obsession. He consumed more than was good for him. One day he became ill, and his parents took him to the doctor.

The doctor's advice was that Anil must drastically reduce the amount of sweets that he consumed. Anil's parents tried to enforce the doctor's orders, but it was difficult because they were relying on parental authority to make Anil obey. Both parents would nag Anil about not eating sweets while they themselves continued to eat sweets every day. Several weeks went by and the parents found that Anil was continuing to eat sweets when no one was looking. They brought him to Grandfather with an appeal to drum some sense into him.

"Anil will not listen to us," his mother told Grandfather. "The doctor has said he should not eat any sweets, but he still consumes them on the sly. He refuses to obey us. Please speak to him."

Grandfather heard the complaint patiently, and just as patiently told Anil's mother, "Come back with Anil after fifteen days."

Anil's mother was perplexed. All she believed Grandfather had to do was tell the boy not to eat sweets. They were bad for him. Why did she have to wait for fifteen days? She could not fathom this, but she was not prepared to argue with Grandfather.

On the fifteenth day she returned. Grandfather took Anil aside and whispered into his ear. Anil's eyes sparkled. Grandfather asked him for a high five to seal their private deal, and they left.

Anil's mother had no idea what had transpired, but she was skeptical. A few days later both parents came back to Grandfather utterly amazed and asked him, "How could Anil obey you so readily, and not us? Tell us the secret."

Grandfather explained, "It was no miracle. I asked you to come back after fifteen days because I had to first give up eating sweets before I could ask him to do so. I simply told Anil that I had not eaten sweets for fifteen days, and that I would not eat any until the doctor allowed Anil to eat sweets."

It was a simple lesson in the power of correcting by example, but how many of us practice this? We are quick to use our authority or superior physical strength to force others to do what we want them to do, and as a result, even if we are obeyed, we have not effected the kind of change that makes our lessons permanent.

I was once the cause of an uproar that some people feared would lead to serious consequences. One day in Pune, as I sat enjoying the cool morning breeze, I felt someone's arm across my shoulder and looked up to see Pundit Jawaharlal Nehru (later elected India's first Prime Minister) smiling down at me.

"Have you had breakfast?" he asked.

"No," I said tentatively. I was overawed to be in such close proximity to the famous political figure, a person who was regarded as second only to Grandfather.

"Would you like to join me?" he asked.

Unable to mask my excitement, I said, "Yes, of course!"

We walked toward the dining room, his arm still around my shoulder. At the table he asked, "What will you eat?"

I was so elated I blurted out, "Whatever you eat."

"That I do not think will be possible," he said. "Your Grandfather will not permit that."

"Why not?" I asked in all innocence. "If you can eat it, why can't I?"

"I am going to eat an omelet," Nehru replied with a smile. "You will have to ask your Grandfather if you want to eat one, too."

"All right. I will go and ask," I said.

I ran right up to Grandfather's room, where he and Sardar V. P. Patel (later elected Deputy Prime Minister) were in the midst of a serious discussion. I barged into the room and cried out, "Bapuji, can I eat an omelet?"

I can still see the surprised look on Grandfather's face as he looked at me. "Have you eaten eggs before?" he asked.

"Yes." I was lying blatantly and I don't know why.

"Well, all right," he said, and went back to his discussion.

I ran back thinking, "That was so easy, I wonder why people make such a fuss over it."

It was the first time I had ever eaten an omelet, and I could hardly finish it. The smell of country eggs was so unpleasant and overpowering to me that I resolved never to eat an omelet again. For strict vegetarians in India, eggs are considered to be non-vegetarian. In the Gandhi family we did not eat any kind of meat, fish or eggs, in part because of Hindu tradition, but also because of Grandfather's belief in nonviolence. At the age of twelve I was quite careless about tradition and philosophy. My thoughts were focused on why Nehru could eat an omelet and I could not.

Some months later, on our way back to Sevagram Ashram, a party including Grandfather, my parents, and a few other people stopped in Bombay where Grandfather had some work. It was decided that we would stay at the Birla House. The vast mansion with its beautiful garden is located on Nepean Sea Road, Bombay's millionaire row. I had never seen or experienced such grandeur and opulence, and so I spent the day exploring every nook and cranny of the palace, as well as the surrounding garden that overlooked the vast expanse of the Indian Ocean. I had still not satisfied my curiosity when Abha called out to me, "Arun, Bapuji wants to see you in his room."

Abha was normally quite jovial and always smiling. At this moment she had a serious look on her face. Placing her arm on my shoulder she said, sympathetically, "You are in big trouble."

"Why? What have I done?" I asked innocently.

"Run to Bapu's room. They are waiting for you," she said, giving me a loving pat on the back.

I ran up two flights of stairs and entered Grandfather's room out of breath. My parents were squatting on the floor with their heads bowed, and Grandfather was quietly spinning and speaking softly to them. The atmosphere was indeed somber, as Abha had warned. Grandfather beckoned for me to come and sit by his side.

"You remember the day in Pune when you asked me if you could eat an omelet?" Grandfather asked.

When I nodded my affirmation he continued. "You told me that you had eaten eggs before, and so I allowed you to eat an omelet. Now your parents deny giving you eggs, so who am I to believe?" His voice was stern but loving.

Hesitating only for a moment, I answered, "But Bapuji, we eat pastries and cakes, and they contain eggs, don't they?"

For a moment there was absolute silence, then Grandfather burst into his famous toothless laugh. "You will be a better lawyer than I ever was. Now run along and play."

There was a collective sigh of relief. Everyone was convinced that Grandfather would do penance, most likely in the form of a fast. Not even my parents thought we would get away so lightly. I am convinced that Grandfather let me off the hook not because I am his grandson, but because in some convoluted sense I had made a legitimate case.

Indeed there were many more incidents that caused Grandfather to react very seriously. One such episode took place in the late 1930s, after he had called upon the people of India to boycott temples that did not allow "untouchables" to worship.

"God can hear your prayers wherever they are uttered," he advised Indians. "You do not need to pray in a temple... I would far rather that Hinduism died than untouchability lived. My fight against untouchability is a fight against the impure in humanity."

In order to spread his message, Grandfather and the entire ashram family began to travel around the country. The tour brought them to the holy city of Jagannathpuri, in Orissa. The Temple of Lord Jagannath, considered one of the four most holy shrines in India, resolutely refused to allow untouchables to enter within its precincts, let alone to worship.

Grandmother Kastur faced a dilemma. As a pious Hindu it was inconceivable for her to be at the doorstep of one of her faith's most important shrines and not go in to worship. There was an internal war between her spiritual needs and her husband's ideological beliefs, and this weighed heavily upon her. This did not mean that she had no commitment to the rights of the Harijans, the untouchables. She valued their rights, but weighed against her own spiritual understanding, she questioned which was the greater sin: abstaining from worship in an important shrine, or violating her husband's vow to publicly support the Harijans.

A small group from the ashram who accompanied Kasturba on a city tour were dismayed when Ba asked the driver to stop outside the Jagannath Temple.

"Ba, you are not thinking of going into the temple, are you?" my mother asked in alarm.

"No, we will just look around," Ba said.

Members of the group quietly offered prayers to stop Ba from doing something rash. Kasturba was like a mother to all of them, and in eastern culture a younger person does not argue with an older person, even when the younger one knows that the older is doing something wrong. At most, one can politely draw the older person's attention to what appears to be a mistake and leave it at that.

Grandmother's friend and long-standing companion, the wife of Mahadev Desai, Grandfather's secretary, accompanied her. They walked around the temple debating the pros and cons of entering. At a certain point their spiritual beliefs at last prevailed, and they went in while the rest of the group watched in dismay.

There is no record anywhere of what the two friends said or thought when they decided to disobey Grandfather's wishes and enter the temple. They had both been with Grandfather long enough to know the consequences. Did Ba feel that Grandfather was unjustified in preventing people from worshipping in such an important temple? Or did she think that Grandfather would consider this action not grave enough for serious reaction? Perhaps she believed she would be able to convince Grandfather that going into the temple was something she just had to do.

That evening when they returned home, Grandmother confessed to Grandfather that she could not resist, and had

indeed entered the holy temple. "I knew you would be un-
happy, but you must forgive me," she pleaded.

Grandfather's anguish was written all over his face. "This
is wrong not only between us, but also morally. How can I
convince the people to stay away from oppressive temples when
I am unable to convince my own wife?"

Grandfather went public with the episode at once and
issued an apology. To atone for the mistake, he decided to fast
for seven days. Not only did Kastur and the entire ashram
family join him in sympathy, so also did thousands around
the country.

While I enjoyed basking in the limelight of Grandfather's
attention, what I enjoyed even more about India was the freedom I experienced from fear and oppression. I no longer had
to worry about being insulted by someone with a different
color skin. For the first time in my life, skin color made no
difference in evaluating my character.

Nevertheless, as a teenager, during the years I lived with
Grandfather, I gave little thought to the pernicious caste system that segregated millions of poor Indians as untouchables.
I knew it was an issue that was close to Grandfather's heart,
but I have always been a "slow starter." It is not surprising
that it was not until much later that I realized why Grandfather made the cleaning of toilets an essential part of ashram
life.

This was, without a doubt, the most unpleasant of all
tasks. The untouchables, who are generally employed to empty

buckets of "night soil," are trapped in an endless cycle. Paid a negligible wage, they are forced into a life of poverty that includes all the miseries that go with it. Poverty and social oppression make it impossible for them to send their children to school. Ignorance and a subhuman life-style remain their lot, from which fifty-five years of independence and constitutional privileges have not rescued them.

"You cannot change people's hearts by law," Grandfather said. "You can only change hearts by love." To make people understand humility, and to educate them in the need to respect all people, high and low, were important objectives of ashram living. It was a humbling experience to carry buckets full of urine and night soil, to empty them in the fields, to cover the holes, and to wash the buckets and replace them for use.

In 1969, the year of Grandfather's birth centenary, former residents of Sevagram gathered for a reunion and shared their memories of life at the ashram. Shriman Narayan, who was then Governor of Gujarat State, related to the congregation how his ambitious ego had been tamed by Grandfather in a nonviolent way. The incident, he said, happened some time in the late 1920s, after he had returned from England with a doctoral degree from the London School of Economics, and was brimming with ideas to change the economy of India.

When he enthusiastically shared some of his ideas with his parents they both said, "Before you do anything, you must first seek the blessings of Bapuji." Grandfather was regarded by many as a holy man, whose blessings for any auspicious beginning were imperative.

Narayan arrived at Sevagram Ashram and enthusiastically repeated his grandiose economic schemes to Grandfather, who listened patiently.

"Now give me your blessings so that I can start my work," Narayan said at the end of his speech.

"Your schemes are wonderful, but first I want you to stay at the ashram for some days and join the group that cleans the toilets. Then we will talk about blessings," Grandfather said.

Narayan was speechless. "How can Bapuji be so inconsiderate?" he thought, "I am a doctor of economics, and he wants me to clean bucket toilets?"

It made no sense to him, and besides, he abhorred doing what he considered dirty, menial work. He had never in his life done anything like this before, and yet he knew he could not argue with Gandhi. He assumed that he would have to quietly do Grandfather's bidding for a day or so to satisfy his "quirks," get his blessings, and then move on to his important duties.

Narayan quickly realized how wrong he was. He had to perform this task twice a day for several days. On the third day Narayan pleaded with Grandfather, "Why are you wasting my time with such mundane work? With my knowledge of economics I can do great things for the country."

"I am aware of what you are capable of doing," Grandfather replied. "When you convince me that you can clean toilets for others with the same enthusiasm that you have for reforming their economic system, I will give you my blessing."

Humility, Grandfather was convinced, is a quality all human beings must learn. Respect and humility go together. Humility is not meekness; it is the opposite of arrogance. "If we could learn that we can see the mighty oak inside the acorn, instead of simply acknowledging the acorn on the mighty oak, we could change the world," Grandfather said.

The British, with their pernicious divide-and-rule politics, exploited the caste system to perpetuate their rule in India. They could easily have eliminated the caste system by modernizing the country's sanitation system, educating the oppressed, and elevating them from a life of poverty and destitution. However, not only did they not modernize the sanitation system; they did not even supply the millions employed to carry buckets of feces and urine with the tools to do their work with some small portion of dignity. Often these workers had to carry leaky buckets for long distances on their heads.

People today wonder why Grandfather did not take more radical public measures to eradicate the caste system. Why did he seem content with seemingly modest changes, such as calling the low castes Harijans ("Children of God"), opening temples for Harijans to worship, and starting schools for Harijan children?

History has largely forgotten that even these simple changes generated such anger that they motivated eight attempts on Grandfather's life. If the changes he proposed roused such strong passions among the powerful Brahmins, what might have happened if he had proposed even more revolutionary changes is frightening to imagine.

Furthermore, changing the name "untouchable" to "Harijan" is not as simple as it appears. Gandhi said, "By their quiet suffering these people have earned the right to be called children of God. The rest of Hindu society will also earn the right to be called children of God when they atone for their past sins."

Clearly, Grandfather looked forward to a day when all Hindus would be known as Harijans, a day when the caste system would be abolished.

Parents' Love
Shravan and the Long Walk to Phoenix

Describing his experiences at Tolstoy Farm, near Johannesburg, South Africa, Grandfather wrote in his autobiography,

> We made it a rule that the youngsters should not be asked to do what the teachers did not do, and therefore when they were asked to do any work, there was always a teacher cooperating and actually working with them. Hence, whatever the youngsters learned they learned cheerfully. . . .
>
> Of textbooks, about which we hear so much, I never felt the want. I do not even remember having made much use of the books that were available. I did not find it at all necessary to load the boys with quantities of books. I have always felt that the true textbook for the pupil is his teacher. I remember very little that my teacher taught me from books, but I have even now a clear recollection of the things they taught me independently of books.
>
> Children take in much more and with less labor through their ears than through their eyes. I do not remember having read any book from cover to cover with my boys. But I gave them, in my own language, all that I had digested from my reading of various books, and I dare say they are still carrying a recollection of it in their minds. It was laborious for them to remember what they learned from books, but what I imparted to them

by word of mouth they could repeat with the greatest ease. Reading was a task for them, but listening to me was a pleasure, when I did not bore them by failure to make my subject interesting. And from the questions that my talks prompted them to put, I had a measure of their power of understanding.

Grandfather taught me many things by word of mouth, drawing stories from his vast storehouse of knowledge and experience. In one of my lessons, Grandfather told a tale of sacrifice and love from ancient mythology that had strongly influenced his own life. It is the story of a young man's devotion to his parents and their devotion to him, which, I believe, reflected Grandfather's strong sense of guilt over not being present at the death of his father and, later, at the death of his mother.

Grandfather was still a teenager when his father became severely ill. One night, until late in the evening, he tended to his bedridden father's needs and massaged his legs. All the while, he says in his autobiography, he was generating erotic fantasies about his young wife, who was alone in another room. Then his father's younger brother arrived and said to Grandfather, "You have done enough for now. I will take over and you can go to bed."

Grandfather said he felt great relief and sped away from his father's bed to his own, where Kastur was trying to sleep. He woke her urgently because he wanted sex. Minutes later there was a knock on his door.

"Who is it?" Grandfather asked impatiently.

"Come quickly, your father is dying," the night nurse called out.

He went to his father's bedside at once, but by the time he arrived his father had passed away. This incident haunted Grandfather all his life, and possibly explains why the following ancient legend meant so much to him.

Shravan was an only child of modest peasants who barely eked out a living. With age, his parents lost their sight, becoming dependent upon their son for all their needs. Shravan tried to make their lives as comfortable as possible.

One day Shravan overheard his mother say to his father that she wished to go on a pilgrimage to the four most holy Hindu shrines in the four geographical corners of India before she died. It was by no means an easy wish to fulfill, since travel in ancient times in India was either by foot, or by an animal-drawn vehicle, such as a buggy or an oxcart.

Fulfilling his mother's wish became for Shravan an obsession. In spite of their economic hardship, Shravan was determined to take his parents on the pilgrimage. He wove two strong baskets and tied one to each end of a strong rod of bamboo. He would carry his parents in this contraption from one shrine to the next.

Wishing to surprise his parents, Shravan planned everything in secrecy. Then, when he had all the details worked out, he told his parents they would set forth on their pilgrimage the following morning.

"But how?" his parents asked incredulously. "We are old

and frail and losing our eyesight, and we cannot even walk."

"Do not worry," Shravan explained. "I will carry both of you in baskets slung across my shoulders." He said it with such finality that there was no more argument.

They left at the crack of dawn for a tour that would take them months, if not years to complete. Shravan walked, rested, slept, ate and walked again for hundreds of miles before they reached the first center. From there they continued to the next. Several months passed in this way, and finally they began the longest portion of the journey, through dense forests to the south. At noon one day, in the thickest part of the forest, Shravan stopped, placed the baskets under a huge tree, and told his mother to prepare for lunch while he went to the stream to fetch some water.

Somewhere in the remote forest King Dasaratha, the father of Lord Rama (an incarnation of the god Vishnu) was hunting with bow and arrow. He was a great marksman who could shoot an arrow in the direction of any sound and hit his target. King Dasaratha heard the sound of water splashing and, assuming it was an animal drinking water at the stream, he shot an arrow into the trees. Instead of the cry of a wounded animal, the king heard the agonized wail of a human being. What had he done?

Shravan was grievously injured. He lay moaning in the mud with the arrow in his back. King Dasaratha carried him up from the river bank and set him down in the grass. Cradling Shravan's head in his lap, the king tried to comfort him.

"I do not know what to say," King Dasaratha told Shravan.

"I did not expect another human being in this part of the forest."

"I am worried about my parents who are old and blind," Shravan whispered. "What will happen to their wish to visit the holy centers?"

"I understand your agony," the king said wretchedly. "I wish I could take the arrow back and save your life. However, I promise that I will take care of your parents and ensure that their every wish is fulfilled."

"You do not know my parents," Shravan said sadly. "If they find out that I am dead they will kill themselves."

"I will try to be to them as good a son as you were," the king murmured.

As he said this, Shravan died in his arms. The grief-stricken king instructed his aides to perform the last rites for Shravan while he carried the pail of water to the old parents, who were growing anxious in their son's absence.

"What kept you so long?" Shravan's mother asked as she heard his footsteps.

The king dared not speak lest she find out that he was not Shravan. "Shravan's silence is unusual," his mother thought. "He never avoids a question."

She asked again and still he refused to answer. She concluded that Shravan must be tired and therefore angry with himself for undertaking such a long journey. As a last resort she said, "We could abandon this pilgrimage and go home, you know." Her son still refused to speak.

The three travelers ate in silence and then continued on

the journey. Since the king, as Shravan, refused to talk, the old couple remained silent as well. They realized they could not do anything to help their son if he refused to talk. Both parents silently wondered what could have happened to him so suddenly. He was so cheerful and talkative until he went to the stream to fetch water.

Late in the day they stopped again. This was the first time that Shravan did not describe to his blind parents the beautiful sights and the activities of the wildlife that surrounded them. The journey became joyless for the old couple. Shravan's silence was bewildering, and therefore, they began to lose interest in their pilgrimage.

When night fell and the king had made beds for the couple, he was faced with a dilemma. How could he assist them through their washing and tuck them into bed without touching them? Shravan had warned him that they would recognize that he was not their son by touch. The king was still grappling with this problem when Shravan's mother said, "Son, give me your hand so that I can get up."

She had noticed that her son had not only stopped talking, but had tried to keep away from them. She was sure once she had a grip on his hand she would be able to make him talk and share his suffering. Reluctantly, King Dasaratha offered his hand and she eagerly grabbed it. Then, just as rapidly, she let go of it. "This is not the hand of my son!" she exclaimed. "Who are you, and where is my son?"

The king realized he could no longer keep up the charade. In a voice full of remorse he narrated the unfortunate incident that killed their son. It was a hunting accident, he explained, but he begged to be allowed to do penance for this sin and fulfill the role of their son, Shravan. Both parents sobbed inconsolably. "Dead?" they exclaimed in disbelief. "Our son is dead and you did not tell us all this time?"

They were shattered and heartbroken. Neither the king's heartfelt remorse nor his promise of a generous compensation could take away the pain of Shravan's parents. In one voice they both declared, "If our son is dead we do not wish to live. Just leave us in this forest so that we can die in peace."

The old couple refused water and food, and the king helplessly watched as they slowly perished.

There were important lessons in this story that Grandfather wished to teach me:

* Never kill or harm another creature.

* Never be so arrogant as to act without looking ahead.

* Honor, love and care for your children and parents, because everything you give to them will be given to you in return.

I was sixteen years old before I fully realized the depth of my father's love for me. I discovered it through an incident that took place after Grandfather's death, while living again with my parents at Phoenix Farm, eighteen miles outside the city of Durban, South Africa.

Phoenix was situated in the middle of nowhere, surrounded by sugar cane plantations with neighbors scattered far and wide. Eighteen miles was a considerable distance in those days, because of bad roads and slow vehicles. It took almost an hour by car to travel from Phoenix to the center of town.

One Saturday my father had to go to Durban to attend a conference, and he did not feel like driving. He asked me, "Would you like to drive me into town today?"

I was still under eighteen, the legal age to get a driver's license in South Africa, but I was big enough to pass for eighteen and a proficient driver.

"Of course," I said enthusiastically. Living in the wilderness of Phoenix did make us lonely. A day in town would give me an opportunity to visit friends and possibly see a movie. My parents, of course, had different ideas about how I would spend the day. Mother gave me a list of groceries she needed and a couple other errands to run, and Father asked me to do some chores for the ashram printing press and to get the car serviced and its oil changed.

"Please attend to these chores, since you have the whole day to yourself," he said.

"Certainly," I said boldly. In my head, I was furiously trying to plan the day so that I could squeeze in at least a movie, if not a meeting with friends. At sixteen, I was fascinated by western movies with Roy Rogers, Gene Autry and John Wayne. I knew these were not the type of movies that my parents would allow me to see, especially since they projected nothing but violence. I kept my plans to myself.

When I dropped Father off at the conference venue, he said, "I will wait for you outside this auditorium at five o'clock this evening. Pick me up here, and we will drive home to-gether."

"Okay," I said, and rushed off to finish my chores in time to make it to a movie.

I left the car at the garage and completed everything else I had been asked to do in time to make the John Wayne double-feature, which started at two o' clock. I was thrilled. My ini-tial plan was to leave during the intermission, but that came at three-thirty. "It is too early to pick up Dad," I said to my-self. "Why not sit a while longer and see part of the second movie?"

Of course I became so engrossed in the second movie that I lost track of the time. It was five-thirty when the movie finally ended, and I ran to the garage to get the car.

I did not reach the auditorium until nearly six o'clock, and Father was understandably worried about my tardiness. "Why are you late?" he asked.

I felt so ashamed to admit that I had spent the afternoon watching two violent western movies that I lied. "The car wasn't ready," I said, and even as the words came out of my mouth I could see the disappointment on Father's face.

"That's not what the garage told me when I called them," he said, getting out of the car again. "I am sorry you lied to me today. Obviously, I did not instill in you the confidence and courage to tell the truth without fear. I must do penance for my shortcoming, so I am going to walk home."

I jumped out of the car and ran after him to apologize, but it was of no avail. He kept walking.

"It is not your mistake," he explained. "It is mine. As your father, I should have given you the courage to tell me the truth, but I failed and I must find out where I went wrong."

I could not walk with Father because I had to bring the car home, nor could I drive away and leave him behind. More than two-thirds of the route to our home were country roads without lights, and it was nearly dark. Consequently, I crawled the car behind Father for five and a half hours, watching him suffer morally and physically because of my dishonesty. Furthermore, I knew mother would be anxious, because she was expecting us home for dinner. In those days communications were difficult. A phone call to locations outside the city could take more than an hour.

My mother spent anxious hours wondering what had happened to us. She spent much of the time on the terrace of the house with my sisters, peering into the dark to see if she could spot our car. When, late into the night, they finally saw headlights creeping ever-so-slowly towards the house, they assumed that we were having some mechanical problem with the car. It was only when we got home that Mother learned what had happened.

I made some hot water and brought a large dish so that Father could soak his tired feet. I apologized to both my parents and promised that I would never lie again.

It is now fifty years since this incident occurred, and not only is it still fresh in my mind, but I often wonder what my reaction would have been if I had been punished. The penance that father did made me feel remorseful enough to promise I would never do it again. Had he punished me, I am sure I would have felt humiliated instead of guilty, and humiliation would have lead to disobedience and revenge.

That my father took the responsibility upon himself to build and nurture a loving relationship, rather than punishing and humiliating, was such a positive experience that I learned a lifelong lesson from it, a lesson in nonviolent parenting that I will never forget.

A Connected World
The Pencil and the Rose

I was not a twelve-year-old genius who instantly understood the meaning or significance of nonviolence. In fact, it was hard to teach me anything. I was very playful and absorbed in games rather than lessons. After growing up, I realized that not many adults had a clear understanding of nonviolence either, so as a young boy, if I did not understand all the nuances of nonviolence, perhaps it was a pardonable lapse.

When I first arrived at Sevagram Ashram, I thought nonviolence simply meant not acting in physically violent ways. Patiently, over a period of time, Grandfather taught me that nonviolence was more expansive than I had realized. To understand the philosophy and be able to appreciate it, he said I must learn to think and behave nonviolently in everything I do. A casual and seemingly harmless incident one day in 1945, while I lived with Grandfather in Pune, communicated this lesson in a way I have never forgotten.

As I was absentmindedly walking home from school, I happened to look down at the little butt of a pencil I carried in my hand. It was dull and scratched, just three inches long, and I thought to myself that it was too small to use anymore. Thoughtlessly, I threw the pencil away into the grass alongside the road, quite certain that Grandfather would give me a new one. Although my parents ensured that I did not waste things that I did not want, I did not expect that throwing away that little pencil would matter very much. But I was wrong. It mattered a great deal.

That evening, during my private time with Grandfather, I told him I needed a new pencil.

"Why do you need a new pencil?" he asked. "You had a perfectly good one this morning."

"It was too small," I argued.

"It did not look too small to me," Grandfather responded. "Let me see it."

"Oh, I threw it away," I said matter-of-factly. I had no idea it was going to be a big issue.

"You threw it away?" he asked.

"Yes," I said meekly.

"In that case you will have to find it," he said.

"Find it?" I asked in shock. "But, Bapuji, how can I find such a tiny pencil in the dark?"

Grandfather found a flashlight. "Take this," he said. "It will help you. I am sure if you retrace your steps and apply your mind you will find it."

There was no possibility of argument. It was not a question of Grandfather forcing me to go look for the pencil. In these kinds of situations he was always able to persuade others that what he said was the right thing to do. I set out off down the road in the dark, peering into the bushes and gutters all along the roadside. I felt ridiculous. Passersby thought I was looking for something important. Some offered to help, but when I told them I was looking for a little pencil stub, they decided not to trouble themselves.

"A little pencil?" one of them asked incredulously. "Is it made of gold?"

It took me two hours to find the pencil. Jubilantly, I rushed back home to show it to Grandfather, hoping that he would now agree that the pencil was indeed too small.

"Good, I am glad you found it," he said, placing the pencil on his little table. "Now, sit beside me and I will explain to you why I made you look for it.

"I am sure you were annoyed that I made you search for a small, seemingly insignificant pencil, but I know it will help you remember your lesson well. Always remember: Wasting anything is a bad habit. Do you know how much money, effort and natural resources go into making things for our use, even pencils? Imagine if millions of people around the world threw away perfectly good pencils each day. How much would it cost the world? Hundreds of thousands of acres of trees are chopped down just for the wood. Add to this the human effort, the money invested, and all the other incidental expenses, and you have an enormous figure. All that goes down the drain every day. That is violence against nature.

"Remember, today it is a pencil that you threw away. Tomorrow you might throw away something else that is of use to someone. So every time you throw something away, ask yourself, 'Can someone use this? Am I justified in throwing it away?'

"The second lesson you need to learn is that when we

overconsume the Earth's resources, we create an economic imbalance in societies and in the world. Affluent people and affluent societies can afford to buy everything in large quantities. They have an abundance of wealth and think they have the license to waste. They use a great deal and leave others with very little. It is this imbalance between the rich and the poor that gives rise to crime, violence, prejudice and other negative attitudes.

"When some people cannot get what they need through honest hard work, and see others wasting what is so precious, they feel justified in taking it by force. The Earth can produce enough for everyone's need, but not for everyone's greed. Our greed and wasteful habits perpetuate poverty, which is violence against humanity.

"I want you to understand the importance of this lesson and why I made you go look for the pencil. Always remember that wasting anything is violence, and every action makes a difference somewhere in the world. You must learn to use everything carefully, sparingly and completely, so that we can share the resources of the world equally with everyone."

I thought the lesson was over, but it was not. Grandfather told me that he was not quite finished with me. "I want you to do an assignment which will teach you more about what I just said. You need to learn about all the different nuances of violence. Ironically, you will understand the depth and scope of nonviolence only after you understand the depth and scope of violence. In other words, it is through understanding violence that you will understand its opposite. Once you understand your own violence, you will be able to do something about it."

My assignment was to construct a "family tree of violence," using the same principles as a genealogical tree. Grandfather instructed me to hang a large sheet of paper on the wall of my bedroom and begin by writing "Violence" as the title, with two subgroups — "Physical" and "Passive."

"Every night analyze what you saw, read, or heard during the day, even things that you may have done to others, and place them under the appropriate headings on the tree. This exercise, regularly done, will teach you the different aspects of violence, and how thoroughly they penetrate our lives."

Physical violence is easy to see and define. It is the type of violence in which physical force is exerted: wars, murders, killings, beatings, rape, and hundreds of other such examples.

Passive violence, on the other hand, can easily be overlooked or justified because it is violence without exerting physical force. Still, it is destructive. Examples of passive violence include all kinds of waste, discrimination, oppression (economic, political, social, cultural, religious, racial, gender), name-calling, gossiping — in other words, any action that hurts others, consciously or unconsciously. When we ignore the poverty of other people and dismiss them as people who can fend for themselves, or when we make the poor dependent upon handouts for their existence, we commit passive violence.

I strongly recommend building a tree of violence to everyone, young and old, as a step towards self-discovery and self-improvement, and ultimately as a means to work for peace in the world. This exercise made me aware of how much violence there is around us, as well as how we contribute to it as individuals. Having to analyze my actions every day was an educational experience and an opportunity for introspection. Once I observed which of my actions were acts of violence, I was prepared to find and practice ways to avoid such violence each day.

This exercise also revealed how close the link was between passive violence and physical violence. When one person inflicts passive violence upon another person and thereby causes suffering, the victim of passive violence is likely, in time, to react in anger using physical violence. Passive violence, therefore, is potentially a fuel that ignites physical violence at home, in our neighborhoods, in society and among nations. How can we put out a fire that we continuously feed with gasoline?

People are living in denial, Grandfather said, when they oppose physical violence alone and claim that they are non violent, and therefore don't need to make changes in their behavior. If we eliminate passive violence in ourselves, and strive toward influencing others wherever we can, we will generate a considerable decline in the amount of violence that prevails in our societies today.

It is tempting to look at the population of the world and say, "I am just one of seven billion people, so what difference can I make?" It was Grandfather's belief that no small action in the cause of peace could be neglected, and that every effort takes us closer to our goal. "We can work through eternity for peace and not achieve anything, as long as we refuse to be the change we wish to see in the world."

Grandfather liked to tell another story that illustrates how small gestures can profoundly effect other people, and contribute to a better world.

There was a hopelessly disorganized young man who lived alone in a small apartment, which was so cluttered and unclean that it resembled a pigsty. He refused to do his own household chores. Layers of dust and dirt covered everything, unwashed clothes were strewn all over, and the kitchen sink overflowed with dirty dishes. He was aware of his poor living conditions but, he argued, if I don't invite anyone home, no one will know.

At work one day he met a lady, and soon they began to develop a relationship. He always made sure he did not take her home. They met outside. Love blossomed, and one day, while walking in the park, his girlfriend plucked a beautiful red rose and gave it to him. It was a gift of love and it had to be preserved with dignity. In his home he could not find a clean vase. He rummaged through all the dirty dishes and discovered one that was unclean and moldy.

He scrubbed the vase clean, filled it with water, and placed the rose of love into it. Now this vase needed a place to be seen in all its beauty. He could not very well put it amid all the mess everywhere.

He decided the dining table in the kitchen was the ideal

spot for the rose, so that he could see it all the time he was at home. This meant that he had to clean up the table. Now the table looked so clean and beautiful that it seemed out of place in the filthy room. So he cleaned the kitchen, washed the dishes, polished the floor, and transformed the kitchen into a bright spot. He felt happy with the transformation, but the kitchen now stood in stark contrast with the rest of his untidy home. So, little by little, he ended up cleaning the whole house. It was one small act of love that transformed an otherwise careless, untidy person.

Approaching others with care and respect makes a great difference. Had anyone known of this man's unpleasant personal habits, a common reaction would have been to criticize him and put him to shame. Sometimes people respond positively to shame, but more often they react rebelliously and perpetuate their unpleasant ways. Compassion and love, which are the cornerstones of Grandfather's theory of conflict prevention and resolution, have the capacity to influence other people more effectively, and with lasting results.

The Spinning Wheel
Humanity, Materialism and Morality

One day during my lesson hour with Grandfather, he asked me to dismantle his spinning wheel. When I did, he said, "Now, spin this cotton sliver into yarn."

"How can I do that," I asked, "when the machine is dismantled?"

"Very well, then, put it together again," he said.

While I was busy doing this he took away a very small wheel. I could not complete the assembly without this wheel, so I asked him for it.

"Why do you need it? It is so small. Can you not make the machine work without it?"

"No, I cannot," I said.

"Exactly," Grandfather said. "Just as the machine cannot function when it is divided into separate parts, life cannot function meaningfully when each person acts independently. Also, just as the smallest wheel is necessary to make the spinning wheel work properly, every individual that God has created is an integral part of the whole, and must work in unison with others so that life can be smooth and in harmony. Nobody is dispensable."

The reason why human society does not function today as efficiently as we would like is because, as individuals and as nations, we neglect the rules that Grandfather illustrated here so simply.

Through his philosophy of nonviolence, Grandfather tried to inspire a sense of morality, and revive, among other things, an awareness that every human is an integral part of life. It is only when we learn to accept and respect every individual, whatever their background, that nonviolence will become meaningful and effective. Respect for others enables us to understand who we are, our proper role in life, and how we can fulfill this role to the benefit of all.

It is difficult for me to believe that hmanity is the end product and ultimate beneficiary of all creation. All other species in nature quietly and diligently fulfill their natural roles and enhance the world, while human beings, regarding ourselves as the most intelligent of species, live in confusion. We continually search for the answer to the question, "What is the meaning of life?" And when we fail to find an easy answer, we proceed as though life means nothing more than amassing personal wealth.

By following this path, our world has become increasingly wedded to materialism. People who successfully pursue their own wealth and comfort while ignoring the needs of others are admired and emulated, and relationships, when they are built at all, are often dependent upon personal advancement and other benefits. Materialism breeds arrogance towards those who have less than ourselves, and exaggerates the economic disparities between human beings. Our needs grow in proportion to our means, and so we consume senselessly and wastefully. Materialism also encourages passive violence against nature, by which we are rapidly destroying our world, with a wishful but mistaken belief that we will always be able to extract what we need.

Grandfather warned that there is an inverse relationship between materialism and morality. As materialism increases, morality decreases. He taught that one's spiritual life is to be valued higher than the accumulation of wealth, and also said that one who has never uttered a prayer, but has served fellow humans with love, respect and nonviolence, is nearer to God than one who prays ten times a day.

Because my parents, Manilal and Sushila, lived a life of non-violence, they were able to build constructive, caring relation-ships with people from every economic, racial, political and religious group they encountered. As I was growing up, I was taught to befriend everyone — from the children of farm-hands and African tribes to those of distinguished guests.

Some of my African friends from very poor families were educated by my parents, my eldest sister and myself. My par-ents encouraged me to teach them whatever I learned in school, so that all our playmates eventually learned to read and write. They learned hygiene. They learned about different people and different countries. In return, the African children shared their skills in traditional crafts, working with wood and clay. We were never allowed to consider ourselves superior by vir-tue of our formal education.

An analysis of conflicts around the world today will readily reveal that they all have roots in the gross lack of respect people have for those with economic, religious, educational, nationalistic or cultural differences. We are adept at finding reasons for hating others. It is this attitude, more than anything else, which contributes to the violence that afflicts humanity today. It was Grandfather's view, passed down to me through my parents, that no one is superior or inferior. No one can assert special rights over another, and no one is an enemy.

When we begin to understand our true role in creation, we begin to see the importance of accepting others. Acceptance changes our perspective on life. With acceptance we cease to classify people. We cleanse our minds of the scourge of discrimination, which allows us to dehumanize certain groups, and then relate to them in a violent manner.

Once we have divested ourselves of all the labels that separate us and begin to look at all people, including ourselves, as human beings, united by common aspirations and a common nature, we will have taken a major leap in the long journey to a nonviolent world. Human society, after all, is like Grandfather's spinning wheel — an assembly of interdependent parts. When every piece is brought together and respectfully maintained, the machine works beautifully. But neglect the smallest wheel and the machine is useless.

Part Three

Lessons from Life

Nonviolence Notebook

Penance and Punishment

Growing up in a nonviolent home, my two sisters and I were not punished in the traditional way. Our parents undertook penance for the wrongs we committed. This penance often took the form of fasting, which, in the Gandhian tradition, meant living only on water. Depending on the severity of the offense, the penance might range from skipping one meal to fasting for one or two days. Before penance was undertaken, there was a family discussion of the misdemeanor and the reasons for the penance.

Through the practice of penance, parents can take responsibility for giving their children a positive upbringing. Punishing children for wrongdoing implies that the children are guilty, that the parents have no responsibility, and that the child, as the guilty party, must suffer. But children do wrong things for many reasons: They don't know better; they are experimenting; they are influenced by others whose behavior seems acceptable to them. Sometimes they see their parents or other adults in the home behaving in a similar way, and feel that if it is all right for adults to do it, then it has to be all right for them, too. Because punishment fails to address any of these issues, it is certain to fail in its purpose.

No Formula To Nonviolence

An important thing to remember in the practice of nonviolence is that one must not be dogmatic. Because Grandfather used method A to effect change in a certain situation, it does not mean that method A can be used in similar situations. In nonviolence there is no formula, as there is in violent solutions, where one can institutionalize fixed responses. This is, perhaps, a shortcoming of the "three strikes and you're out" rule of American criminal justice. Nonviolence requires one to be innovative, to shape one's response according to each unique set of circumstances. The possibilities are endless.

An Eye for an Eye

In western society justice has come to mean revenge, "an eye for and eye." It is so ingrained in us that we do not have a sense of closure unless someone is made to pay for their wrongdoing. For centuries, humans have controlled one another by fear. The greater the fear, the greater the control. Yet, "An eye for an eye," Grandfather said, "only makes the whole world blind."

The Word "Enemy"

The word "enemy" does not exist in the vocabulary of nonviolence. Even the British, who ruthlessly captured, oppressed and exploited the people of India economically and politically, were not considered enemies.

Understanding and Aggression

We generate conflicts when we have little or no respect for others, and when we are primarily concerned about our own desires and demands. We aggravate conflicts by injecting anger and aggression into our relationships rather than using our energy to find positive and equitable solutions. Learning to build and nurture good relationships with others, including those who challenge us, is a prerequisite to a nonviolent way of life.

A recent political situation in the southern United States, I believe, sheds light on this principle. I am referring to the widely-publicized controversy over the use of the Confederate flag. The NAACP — the National Association for the Advancement of Colored People — has spearheaded for some years a nonviolent campaign to disallow any public display of the Confederate flag. While they have succeeded in some places, they have created ill will in others. In Mississippi, for example, the feelings among whites and blacks over the issue escalated so high that it lead to a statewide political referendum, in which two thirds of the votes were cast in favor of retaining the Confederate flag.

I believe there were two things that went wrong in the NAACP's campaign. First, although the NAACP were not physically violent in their approach, they were very aggressive. Second, they lost sight of their ultimate purpose, which is to create and nurture harmony between whites and blacks in the United States. If the goal is to achieve true integration in the hearts of the people of the nation so that all can live with dignity and freedom, then aggressively fighting over a symbol is perhaps the wrong way to achieve it.

The issue of the Confederate flag seems to have only grown more bitter. Now that the die has been cast, the NAACP will have to take the battle to a new level, and the escalation could go on until one side or the other is legally restrained, or too tired to continue the fight. Neither of these outcomes will be a lasting victory.

Proactive and Reactive Nonviolence

In order to operate successfully, nonviolence must be both proactive and reactive. Reactive nonviolence gained prominence through Grandfather and Dr. Martin Luther King Jr., who acted in response to the discrimination they encountered in their societies. Grandfather reacted first to the prejudices in South Africa, and later to British colonialism in India. Dr. King reacted to racism in the United States.

Grandfather's use of proactive nonviolence in South Africa and India received much less attention from the public. In its proactive mode nonviolence involves cultivating the sensibilities and compassion needed to respect others and their needs so that we can live in harmony. In South Africa, for example, while acting against discriminatory laws and practices nonviolently, Grandfather worked to improve everyday relationships between whites and nonwhites in order to avoid future conflicts. Similarly, in India he tried to improve relations between Hindus and Muslims, between high castes and low castes, between the rich and the poor.

According to Grandfather, the proactive mode of non-violence involves "trusteeship," which means that, individually and collectively, we are trustees of the talents and resources that we have and not the owners. Our responsibility is to use them for the benefit of all.

In our selfish mode we consider ourselves owners of these things and, therefore, we exploit them for personal gain. This selfishness causes friction among people, leading eventually to conflict. If, however, we share our talents and resources intelligently, and help one other to attain our common and individual goals, we will create lasting peace.

The Five Elements of Nonviolence

Whether used proactively or reactively, a fundamental principle of nonviolence is to bring about better relationships between the oppressed and the oppressor, through what I have sometimes described as "The Five Elements of Nonviolence": love, respect, understanding, acceptance and appreciation.

Gandhi and King succeeded in their objectives to a large degree by applying these elements. It would be a mistake to suppose that they were successful because they were contending with kind, compassionate or conscientious opposition. Ruthless attempts were made to crush their movements in India and in the United States, and both, ultimately, sacrificed their lives to their causes. Nevertheless, by their quiet, patient and sincere suffering in the face of gross injustice they both brought about deep and lasting transformation in their societies.

Laws and Transformation

To outlaw discrimination and oppression laws are necessary, but by no means sufficient. It is the nature of human beings to resent control by force. Any attempt to impose moral obligations upon unwilling people will lead to two reactions. The first will be "tolerance" by those who don't want to put up a fight. The second will be counter-aggression by those who resent forceful conversion.

For any law to be effective, Grandfather said, it must first have moral appeal. For the most part, people refrain from stealing not because they are afraid of breaking the law, but because they know it is morally wrong to take what does not belong to them. Many of the same people will ignore seat belt laws, because they attach no moral obligation to their observance.

When people are forced to respect civil rights and human rights or face legal consequences, they don't like it. Civil rights laws will be scrupulously observed only when people accept that it is morally wrong to oppress or discriminate against fellow human beings. That awareness can come only through education. A law will enable integration in public places, but it does not foster understanding or appreciation in the hearts of people who continue to live with their prejudices.

The only way, Grandfather concluded, to achieve respectful relationships is through the transformation of the heart. Violence and law are useless in this effort. "You can change people's hearts by love," he said "never by law."

Apple Seeds and Oranges

The basis for Grandfather's belief in the philosophy of non-violence lies in the Hindu conviction that all people are endowed with good and bad qualities. If we appeal to a person's bad qualities, then what emerges is conflict and violence and, on the other hand, if we appeal to good qualities, then what emerges is compassion and understanding. The proof of this can be seen every day.

When we yell or curse at someone, we get the same in return. On the other hand if we love and show compassion to even the most hard-hearted, he or she will ultimately respond with goodness. We cannot plant an apple seed and expect to reap oranges.

Tolerance

In recent decades we have emphasized the value of teaching people "tolerance." Tolerance is not only inadequate, it is a negative concept which only alienates society further. Learning to tolerate absolves people of the responsibility of learning to understand different people, accept and appreciate their differences, and progress towards respecting them for who and what they are. It is only when we build acceptance between people that we will rid ourselves of the scourge of prejudice and liberate ourselves from violence.

Respect for the Family

"If there is no respect for the family," Grandfather said, "there can be no respect for the society." A society is only as loving and cohesive as its families. The family structure in modern times is going through a metamorphosis. Individuals are becoming more independent and more self-centered, because human life as a whole is tainted by materialism. Success is measured in terms of material possessions, and consequently, we teach our children to get to the top by any means possible.

In too many cases, marriages have become meaningless. Sex and materialism have become the most important aspects of life. To get a satisfactory dose of each, people are willing to break marriages and relationships easily. Raising a family was once the reason for two people to get married and stay married. Now many children are simply by-products of a sexual alliance.

In 1988, still new to the United States, my wife and I were given a ride by a young couple that was headed for a holiday. They were so ecstatic that we thought they were newly married and going on their honeymoon. We learned during the conversation that they had been married for five years and that they had a three-month old baby. They felt that they needed to get away from the baby and have some time for themselves.

"Oh, so you are among the lucky few who have a family to take care of the baby while you are on holiday," my wife, Sunanda, commented.

"No," said the lady. "The baby is with a nanny."

"Then, you are fortunate to have a nanny you know and trust to take care of your baby while you are away," Sunanda persisted.

"Well, in fact," said the lady. "we advertised for one and she was hired the day before we left."

To a couple of Easterners this was unthinkable. We have since heard parents talk openly of looking forward to the day when their children would grow up and leave the house so that they could have more time for their own lives. We need to reevaluate such attitudes if we are serious about building a strong society.

Moral Strength and Political Power

Grandfather could use penance as a means to reform a nation of millions because, by his moral strength, he had earned the love of the Indian people. When they indulged in acts of violence in order to advance the cause of independence, he could, by fasting, persuade the people to stop and repent.

The difference between Mohandas Gandhi as a political leader and the President of the United States as a political leader is simply that Gandhi was powerful because of his moral strength, while Presidents have been powerful, with very few exceptions, because of military strength. Without the United States' armed forces, the President would have a severely limited level of influence in the world.

If a nation were to practice "politics with principles," Grandfather said, it would be able to build positive, constructive relationships with people everywhere, and would not have to depend on martial force to maintain its position in the world.

Nehru and the Ram Rajya

There were many Indian leaders, even those close to Grandfather, who were not deeply committed to the philosophy of nonviolence, and abandoned it once independence had been achieved. Jawaharlal Nehru and the Congress Party leaders followed Grandfather during the nonviolent revolution because they had no alternative. None of them had the capacity to inspire the masses as Grandfather did. But when political freedom became imminent, Nehru, speaking on behalf of the Party and the nation, categorically rejected nonviolence as a state policy.

The explanation Nehru gave was that, to Grandfather, a nonviolent society would be "Ram Rajya." Ram Rajya literally means "a state ruled by Lord Rama," an incarnation of the Hindu god Vishnu, who is revered as the model of a selfless, honest and loving ruler. Nehru implied by this that Grandfather wanted to create a Hindu nation. That was a distortion of the truth. By the term Ram Rajya, Grandfather meant that India might someday be a land of equality, justice and prosperity.

It is apparent is to me that Grandfather was a political leader more than a spiritual leader. Someone once suggested that he was a spiritual leader posing as a political leader. He responded, "On the contrary, I am a political leader posing as a spiritual leader." To convince the poor and uneducated masses of rural India, he spoke the language they understood.

The peasants of India belong to three major religions — Hindu, Muslim and Christian — but they are all aware of the story of Lord Rama and Ram Rajya. Such stories have been passed down through the ages in India, and are more widely known than the alien concepts of socialism, democracy and capitalism. When Grandfather talked of creating Ram Rajya, it was to ensure that peace, justice and prosperity were paramount, and would be upheld at all cost.

Nehru interpreted Grandfather's statement in a way that was never intended. It is hard to believe that someone who was so close to Grandfather did not understand his meaning. Throughout his life Grandfather was aware of the composition of the Indian society and worked hard to bring about unity among all — Hindus, Muslims, Christians, low castes, upper castes, and so forth. Could such a person demand a Hindu India?

I do not believe that Nehru misunderstood Grandfather's intentions. He took the position he did because, even before India achieved independence from Great Britain in 1948, he felt that corruption, nepotism and injustice were already so ingrained in Indian political life that creating a Ram Rajya was virtually impossible.

Violence Against Property

For Jayaprakash Narayan, a young Indian revolutionary in the 1930s and 40s, the rationale for disagreement with Grandfather was different than that of Nehru. Narayan was young and brash, and he believed then — as many do today — that nonviolence means not being violent toward other human beings. Violence against property, in his view, was permissible. If someone was injured or killed by the explosion of a bridge or the destruction of railroad tracks, that was indirect and, therefore, forgivable. This is an error.

Today several groups around the world, professing allegiance to nonviolence, use the same kind of arguments. They destroy property and disrupt activities while protesting, and they find, like Narayan did seventy years ago, that their action evokes anger, prejudice and violent responses rather than understanding and empathy. The basis of Gandhi's nonviolence is to appeal to the good in others and evoke sympathy to one's cause through self-suffering.

Common people who are not directly involved in social debates and political conflicts have their lives to live. They need to go to work, take their children to schools, take the ailing to hospitals, and have daily urgent priorities to deal with. When their life is disrupted by someone protesting against injustice or poverty or animal rights or any of the other admirable causes in the world, they become angry at those who are disturbing their lives or damaging property that has to be repaired using public funds. Thus the average person, whose support is often necessary for lasting success, is alienated. Rather than leading to a resolution, they escalate the conflict and create more deeply entrenched opponents.

Nonviolence and Criminal Justice

How can the principles of nonviolence be applied to the criminal justice system today? It is important to remember that nonviolence requires the establishment of a positive relationship between individuals, while punishment does not. In fact punishment ultimately breaks, rather than builds relationships.

Obviously, relationships do not exist between strangers, whether inside or outside prison, but if there is respect for all people, then our attitude towards those who break laws and get into trouble will be different.

Today, because our goal is to punish criminals so severely that they never do anything wrong again, we have to dehumanize them. Once we have reduced them to less than human, we can then do anything we like with them without feeling guilty. If we were to accept them as humans who have been misled by circumstances to do wrong things, then criminal justice would take on a new dimension, and prisons could become places of transformation rather than places of punishment.

The principles of nonviolence suggest that we make prisons into centers of specialized education and rehabilitation so that prisoners can get psychiatric and psychological support from the moment they arrive. Additionally, the education programs in prisons should be more comprehensive than simply offering Graduate Equivalency Degree courses. Classes should be introduced that correspond to the talents of inmates and that can turn their aptitudes toward realistic careers once they return to society.

For several years I have been corresponding with prisoners in various parts of the country through the M. K. Gandhi Institute for Nonviolence, which also runs an annual essay competition inviting prisoners to write their thoughts on nonviolence. When I propose to prisoners that they learn nonviolence so that they can change their lives, they understandably ask, "Why should we change when society has already condemned us? We are never going to get a second chance!"

How could they respond differently? Many prisoners seem to feel that they are on a slippery slope that leads nowhere but down. This would make some kind of sense if we were certain that they were never going to come out of prisons. However, many of them are going to come out and, when they do, they are both more physically powerful, having spent years in prison working out in well-equipped gymnasiums, and more angry, because they hold society responsible for the loss of their self-respect.

The consequences of this and other violent ways of modern societies is that the nations of the world are now forced to spend an inordinately large proportion of their limited financial resources to build and update prisons, military forces and arsenals to preserve their security. The devastating cycle will never end so long as violent means are accepted as a solution to crime.

Halfway House

I was recently called upon to conduct a series of workshops in nonviolence for former prison inmates who had completed their term and had to live in a halfway house before moving into society. At the first workshop, as an icebreaker, I asked the participants to share childhood experiences.

All the thirty-eight men and women in attendance had been victims of drug or alcohol abuse. The group was almost equally divided between the genders and the races, and 90% claimed they started drugs and/or alcohol at the age of nine or ten.

I was aghast. In my naivete I could not fathom how they could indulge in such habits at that young an age. I told them and they laughed. I shared my own experience growing up, when at fifteen I became a victim of peer pressure and started smoking cigarettes. For us this was bad enough. My friends and I had to hide all vestiges of this bad habit by washing ourselves before going home. At least in my case I knew that my parents would never punish me, but they would be hurt and would do penance for my lapse. I did not want to hurt my parents.

So I asked the group, "If I was so afraid of facing my parents smelling of cigarette smoke, how could you face your parents after doing drugs and alcohol?"

There was laughter in the room. Many of the group concurred, "It was our parents who introduced us to drugs and alcohol."

It became clear to me that the problem of violence was

more deeply rooted in the family than I had realized. I found the revelation disturbing at the time, but I am grateful to have learned something that helps me to understand and accept many of those whom society has ostracized.

Empty Drums

Respect and humility go together. Humility is not meekness, but the opposite of arrogance. A wise old Indian man once said," Empty drums make the loudest noise." Grandfather often repeated this phrase to indicate that those with the least understanding are the most arrogant.

Legacy of Love

As we contemplate the world around us, it may seem that we have inherited a legacy of social injustice and domestic and international violence that has sunk to irretrievable depths. One may reasonably ask, "Will it ever be possible to build a world free of hate and prejudice?"

Grandfather's answer to this question could not be simpler or more sincere. "Change is possible if we have the desire and the commitment to make it happen."

We are surrounded by many things that were once considered to be impossible, things that we now take for granted. These things have become part of our lives because someone refused to accept the common wisdom. If this is possible in the material and technological sense, it is equally possible in the moral sense.

Grandfather said, "We must be the change we wish to see in the world." Beginning with ourselves, we must cause positive change to radiate out into the world. We need a change of heart, a change of perceptions, and a change of attitude, which we can then pass on to others through education, enlightenment and love.

About the Author

ARUN GANDHI, the fifth grandson of India's late spiritual leader, Mohandas Karamchand Gandhi, was born in 1934 in Durban, South Africa. Growing up under South Africa's apartheid for someone of Indian heritage was difficult and often dangerous. Enduring attacks from European-African youths for not being "white," and from Native Africans for not being "black" served to fuel the anger that Arun Gandhi bore as a young man. Hoping that time with his grandfather would help the twelve-year-old Arun control his rage and deal with prejudice through nonviolent means, his parents took him to India to live with Mahatma Gandhi in 1946.

Arun's stay with his grandfather coincided with the most tumultuous period in India's struggle to free itself from British rule. His grandfather showed Arun firsthand the effects of a national campaign for liberation carried out through both violent and nonviolent means. For eighteen months, while Gandhi imparted lessons to his grandson, the young man also witnessed world history unfold before his eyes. This combination set Arun on a course for life. His journey was strengthened by the resolve of his parents, Sushila and Manilal, Gandhi's second son, to raise their children according to the principles of nonviolence — including loving discipline (not punishment) shared by child and parent, and lifelong commitment to social progress through nonviolence.

Arun's father, Manilal, spent over fourteen years in prisons as he was repeatedly jailed for his efforts to change South African apartheid nonviolently. Arun's mother, Sushila, spent fifty-four years at Gandhi's ashram, Phoenix, outside Durban. After the deaths of Gandhiji and Manilal, Sushila was the ashram's driving force. She greatly lamented the ashram's physical destruction in 1985, although she asserted the indestructibility of spirit that had created and sustained the community for over eighty years.

At the age of twenty-three Arun returned to India and worked as a journalist and reporter for *The Times of India*. He, his wife Sunanda, and several colleagues started the successful economic initiative, India's Center for Social Unity, whose mission is to alleviate poverty and caste discrimination. The Center's success has now spread to over 300 villages, improving the lives of more than 500,000 rural Indians.

Dr. Gandhi has written eight books and hundreds of articles, He published the *Suburban Echo*, a weekly, in Bombay from 1985 through 1987. He is also the editor of *World Without Violence: Can Gandhi's Dream Become Reality?*, a collection of essays and poetry from noted international scientists, artists, and political and social leaders on the ideals of nonviolence, published in October 1994 for the celebration of the 125th anniversary of Gandhiji's birth.

Arun and Sunanda came to the United States in 1987 to compare race issues in the American South, color discrimination in South Africa, and the caste system in India. In October of 1991 the Gandhis founded the M. K. Gandhi Institute for Nonviolence. The Institute is located at Christian Brothers University in Memphis, Tennessee, where Arun is also a scholar-in-residence.

The M. K. Gandhi Institute for Nonviolence

The M. K. Gandhi Institute for Nonviolence was founded in 1991 by Arun and Sunanda Gandhi to promote and apply the principles of nonviolence locally, nationally and globally, in order to prevent violence and resolve personal and public conflicts. The Institute's efforts focus on conflict prevention, anger management, and relationship- and community-building.

Local programs sponsored by the Institute are aimed at people of all ages, from preschoolers to adults. The Institute is also involved with residents and workers at regional correctional institutions, in a spirit of "being the change we wish to see."

Internationally, the Gandhi Institute works with many organizations dedicated to nonviolence, and Arun 's public presentations have spurred the creation of nonviolence groups throughout the United States.

The Gandhi Institute's work redoubles as the prevention and healing of violence becomes an ever-increasing need in the world. It recalls the prophetic nature of Mahatma Gandhi's statement: "Undreamed of and seemingly impossible discoveries will be made in the field of nonviolence."

For more information, please contact:

M. K. Gandhi Institute for Nonviolence
c/o Christian Brothers University
650 East Parkway, South
Memphis, TN 38104
Email: gandhi@cbu.edu
Internet: www.gandhiinstitute.org